Creating Community

Finding Meaning in the Place We Live

A Handbook
for Comprehensive Community Development

by George Randall West

CREATING COMMUNITY
FINDING MEANING IN THE PLACE WE LIVE

Copyright © 2012 Canadian Institute of Cultural Affairs

All rights reserved. No part of this book may be used or reproduced by any means, graphic, electronic, or mechanical, including photocopying, recording, taping or by any information storage retrieval system without the written permission of the publisher except in the case of brief quotations embodied in critical articles and reviews.

iUniverse books may be ordered through booksellers or by contacting:

iUniverse
1663 Liberty Drive
Bloomington, IN 47403
www.iuniverse.com
1-800-Authors (1-800-288-4677)

Because of the dynamic nature of the Internet, any web addresses or links contained in this book may have changed since publication and may no longer be valid. The views expressed in this work are solely those of the author and do not necessarily reflect the views of the publisher, and the publisher hereby disclaims any responsibility for them.

Written by: George Randall
West Edited by: Karen Snyder Troxel and Ken Gilbert
Cover and book design: Ilona Staples
Cover photograph: Bill Staples

ISBN: 978-1-4620-8963-5 (sc)
ISBN: 978-1-4620-8965-9 (ebk)

Printed in the United States of America

iUniverse rev. date: 12/23/2011

Contents

Foreword

This book is dedicated to the two thousand souls who participated in the research and demonstration of community development in 24 communities one in each of the 24 time zones across the globe. Sponsored by the Institute of Cultural Affairs (ICA), the work began in Chicago in 1965 and continues today in various countries. This book is a distillation of wisdom gleaned from their work and reflection.

The ICA is a private, not-for-profit organization concerned with the human element in world development. Its primary objective is to release the creativity of human beings so they can assume responsibility for their destiny, by empowering individuals, communities, and organizations to find their own solutions and the means to implement them, sometimes referred to as 'bottom-up development'.

The reflections in this book are what I wish I had in 1965 when I walked into the west side, inner city of Chicago for my first experience in an intentional effort to create community. I hope that those on the journey of creating community will find the reflections helpful, if not as a guide, then as something to bounce against to deepen their own insights and intuitions. We began with the conviction that development had to be bottom up, that all the people must be involved, that all the problems had to be addressed, and that operating images blocking individual self-esteem had to be overcome. These were great principles. However a somewhat larger context would have been helpful. Hence this book.

CREATING COMMUNITY

Universal Need

It is self-evident that every human needs community to live full and healthy lives. From the moment of conception, the human baby cannot survive without community to provide its biological needs. It does not thrive without the loving care of community. Likewise, people of all ages need community to 'survive' as authentic, complete human beings. Our need for community is at least as great as the baby's need. We need community for stimulation, for guidance, for an operating context, for knowing ourselves, for acceptance, for correction, for relating us to the larger universe of which we are a part.

We do not know ourselves as individuals without the feedback of other persons. We do not know ourselves as family without the presence of other families in the larger community. The family provides an operating context for knowing ourselves as individuals. The community immediately beyond the family provides the context within which we are aware of ourselves as family. The family and local community provides a framework of values, morals and mores which enable us to discern what is the appropriate action needed in a given situation. The community 'tells' us how to dress, how to walk, how to talk, how to be a person. We may rebel or seek to change the communities operating perceptions; but we must have a place from which to become aware. In order to rebel we must have a community against which to rebel.

Community connects us to the larger universe by providing a specific, concrete 'not me' relationship that enables one to imagine being related to all of creation. It enables us to conceive of ourselves related to the state, nation, world, and the universe. The sense of being a part of the whole universe is extrapolated from the experience of relating to the local, concrete community, without which, the sense of the universal is only an abstraction.

Community allows us to grasp the significance that comes from being a part of something larger than our individual destiny, something bigger than our concern for ourselves and ourselves. It extends the meaning of our lives beyond the span of our lifetime and beyond our limited desires and cares.

Only in relation to the whole, do we experience ourselves fulfilled. A specific, tangible connectedness to the universe enriches our sense of meaning and significance, our sense of being authentic human beings, of having a place in the universe of meaning. All relatively sane human beings desire to be a part of community, to belong, to relate, to communicate with the world outside ourselves, and to be a part of the larger universe.

PART ONE

The Essentials for Successful Formation

The passages between some mountains have to be traversed on tiptoe when they are heavy with snow because a small noise can launch a huge avalanche. Sometimes an avalanche can be caused by the simple act of whistling. In community formation there are actions that are 'whistle actions', creating landslides of favorable results. This section introduces seven 'whistles' that can be blown any time and any place to produce avalanches of community creation. They are the keys to successful formation of healthy community. They are:

1. Interchange. To be a community, people must *respect* and *trust* each other. If they are lucky they may even learn to like one another. Although desirable, liking is not absolutely essential for community formation; but respect and trust are indispensable. To achieve respect and trust requires interchange. It requires face to face interaction, exchange and all forms of sharing. Interchange creates mutual respect, and trust and maybe friendships.

2. Awakenment. To be a community, residents must *assume responsibility* for the community. Responsibility arises from awakening to an *awareness* that calls us to respond. Awareness is the foundation upon which responsibility is built. Until we are aware of the issues facing the community and possible options, we are not able to responsibly respond to and for the community. An *awakened consciousness* jars loose avalanches of responsibility and creative actions tumble into place from many unsuspected places.

3. Demonstration. In genuine community people are *open* and *courageous* to be able to grow, to change and to embrace new possibilities. This is best facilitated by selected demonstrations of possibility that encourage the residents to hope for a better future. Hope in the future is an affirmation of confidence in one's self and the benevolence of creation. Seeing new creations take shape in front of one's eyes releases the courage to believe in a possible future and the courage to risk and trust in one's ability to realize one's dreams.

4. Education. Everyone needs to experience that their efforts are effective, that they are able to accomplish what they set out to do. This means that we all need continuing education as part of a 'learning community' that constantly updates its information and methods of operating. Education allows us to take more control of our life and experience the satisfaction of achieving our goals.

5. Storytelling. A vital community always births a unique and meaningful *identity*. This primarily involves telling a *story* about what is uniquely meaningful about one's community – its gifts, its lure, its value, its contribution to civilization. It is creating a sacred history of the expended lives that formed the community. A good story releases a flood of motivation and a sense of direction and purpose.

6. Direct Action. The community must elicit from its residents a profound *commitment* to the community. This is best realized by direct action of caring for the community that deepens existing commitment and fosters new commitments. When we actively care for someone or some thing, we become attached to that for which we care. When we expend precious time and energy for something, we develop self-interest in the well-being of that for which we gave of ourselves. Commitment flows out of the physical act of caring.

7. Care Forces. Every community needs *stability* and direction, a sense of being in control of its destiny. Self-consciously established care forces – leaders, workers, enablers, and associates – are needed to establish stability. These forces need to be *nurtured*. Leaders are strong when they have caring followers that appreciate and support them. In enabling leaders and workers to be effective, the whole community shares the community responsibilities, sensing that "we are all in this together."

Any program, event or activity that embodies one or more of these 'whistles' facilitates the formation of genuine community in any location anywhere. The 'whistles' are universal necessities for the care and nurture of human beings, catalyzing creativity in all spheres of community and enlivening life in general.

To maximize effectiveness the seven 'whistle actions´ all need to be done at once. They depend on each other. Many activities blow several whistles simultaneously. They supplement and support each other to create the desired avalanche. With careful attention to them, community will happen. Keep them in mind when creating community. These seven whistle actions are the subject of Part One.

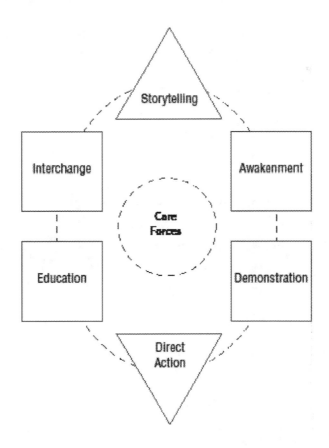

I. INTERCHANGE

Toward Respect and Trust

A. The Interchange Experience

B. Treasures of Interchange

1. Integration of community
2. Breaking barriers
3. Molding character
4. Opening new possibilities
5. Education and training

C. How to Facilitate Interchange

1. Enhance existing interchange
2. Ambience
3. Space
4. Nodes
5. Community events
6. Common planning
7. Work projects
8. Organizations
9. Victory and failure
10. Indirect communication

D. In The Absence of Interchange

E. The Larger Interchange

The *power* of interchange is indisputable.

Interchange of information led to the resignation of one United States president and impeachment procedures against another. It is no accident that dictatorial tyrants fear a free press and free assembly, either of which can remove control from their hands. The right of free assembly and free press are powerful 'interchange rights' and a cornerstone to democratic governance.

Anyone who uses the Internet can attest to how it has changed their relation to friends, family and the world. The Internet has changed the way business is conducted across the globe, not to mention education and scientific research. Can it be only since 1990 when Tim Berners-Lee created the Internet? Think of how other things, like the telegraph, telephone, radio, and television, have impacted the world.

Interchange has launched historical movements, facilitated scientific discoveries, and enabled social breakthroughs, ethical advances, healings, and wars, not to mention the avalanches of great love affairs.

A. THE INTERCHANGE EXPERIENCE

Interchange happens anywhere and any time people get together and share something about which they care. It is especially fruitful for community formation when the shared item is something that is important to the whole community. Interchange is experienced as exchange, interaction, sharing, engagement, and networking.

- **Exchange** includes the exchange of ideas, opinions, views, perspectives, insights, facts, process tools, methods, issues, and possibilities.
- **Interaction** can happen, one with another, one with the group, groups with groups, all with the whole, face to face and indirectly. It is interacting in life-giving events with others from sports to elections. It is celebrating special days, victories and defeats. It is working and playing together.
- **Interchange** can include *sharing* of cares and concerns, joys and sorrows, dreams and hopes, successes and failures, births and deaths. It is sharing

what works and what does not work. It is telling stories of meaningful events and experiences.

- **Personal engagement** is valued above all else. It may be a meeting of minds, or a struggle between two honored adversaries. Stressful or peaceful, it is engaging and deepens relationships.
- **Interchange** establishes useful *networks* across borders of sex, religion or race. It is a sharing of our common humanity with each other, integrating the community into a common human reality, a unifying bond.

B. TREASURES OF INTERCHANGE

1. Integration of Community
Interchange creates within one a sense of being an integral, concrete part of a specific community by creating person-to-person relationships. When you relate to another human being, that relationship connects you to all the relationships of the other person's family, community, city, and nation. It is similar to marrying someone from another country and becoming a citizen of two countries. It builds commitment to others beyond the specific person with whom one is sharing, thus nurturing the spirit of commitment to the whole community.

2. Breaking Barriers
Interchange breaks down barriers of prejudice and ignorance – real or imagined. The prejudice that existed in the United States against the 'black Irish' broke down while the prejudice against the black African American population continued. Since one could not immediately identify a 'black Irishman' by the color of his skin, interchange happened before people were aware that they should be prejudiced, and they discovered most Irish people were actually quite charming.

3. Molding Character
Witnessing the courage, faith and endurance of others strengthens us. We adopt role models from those we admire. When the interior being is altered, all of the outside relations are rearranged. In one inner city community

the depression of the youth seemed insurmountable. Staying 'doped out' seemed to be the appropriate response to their situation. A program was begun that set up a dialogue between the youth and great African Americans like Fredrick Douglas, Martin Luther King, Malcolm X, and Dick Gregory. In the interchange with these great men, the participants began to alter their attitudes. These youth set aside pot and took up the mission of renewing their community. When their interior life changed, their posture changed and many new possibilities rose before them.

4. Opening New Possibilities
Interchange opens windows of new opportunities and creates a willingness to try new things. When one hears of something succeeding elsewhere, one is likely to be more willing to try something new.

In Africa twenty communities were invited to assist each other in their own development. A monthly interchange meeting became the key to their success. Following a formal training program called DOOP ('Do Our Own Project'), community leaders met monthly to exchange ideas and report on their victories. Invariably, when someone reported a success in one community, other communities would say in effect, "We can do that!" and off they would go and do it. This monthly interchange made it possible to assist the development of twenty villages with the same number of staff used to assist a single village in other settings.

5. Education and Training
We acquire a lot of our knowledge and our abilities from seeing others do things. We learn from others how to accomplish different tasks, how to think and plan, and how to understand or relate to a situation. Interchange also teaches us how to relate to others, how to communicate, how to form friendships and alliances, how to negotiate compromises. Interchange increases our ability and willingness to share with others our wisdom, knowledge, and abilities. In sharing our wisdom we share ourselves and learn to trust our fellow human beings. In sharing we open ourselves to understanding others and ourselves.

C. HOW TO FACILITATE INTERCHANGE

1. Enhance Existing Interchange
The first approach to facilitating interchange is to enhance existing interchange in the community. If there are regular meetings and activities that are happening, then do whatever is necessary to enhance the experience of those events. Enable them to be more meaningful, more enjoyable, more lively, more likely to attract more people to participate.

2. Ambience
If the setting is chaotic or sterile, then interchange is diminished. If the setting is inviting and as comfortable as possible within the given limitations, the interchange is more effective. A pastor in Washington, D.C. noted that most church rooms negate interchange between people. He claimed the church was missing an opportunity because it did not create an atmosphere that encouraged genuine interchange. He thought that the local bar was a better place to relax and have a serious conversation with another human being. Designers of bars and lounges know that the seating, lighting and decoration profoundly affect the way we relate to other persons. An appropriate ambience considerably improves the desired results of an event, making the event more enjoyable, more productive, and more rewarding, by creating an inviting atmosphere where ideas and experiences are easily shared in an attractive setting.

3. Space
The order and structure of space is also important to interchange. If you go to a meeting where chairs are set in rows, interchange is immediately discouraged and limited because the room arrangement invites the participants to be quiet and listen. If the chairs are in a circle, the space invites the participants to share among themselves. They are much more likely to enjoy significant interchange. Interchange can be improved simply by the appropriate arrangement of the space.

4. Nodes
Nodes are an important facilitator of interchange. Every healthy community

has places where people naturally gather and share with others. It could be the sports field, a shady tree, a bus stop, a neighborhood store, a park bench, street corner, swimming hole, bath house, bar, restaurant, bakery, ice cream parlor, drugstore or pizza shop. Local markets are often nodes of interchange where people, in the midst of their daily shopping, stop for a few words of conversation with the sellers and other buyers. Wherever people go to eat or drink and visit with other people is an important interchange opportunity.

Improving the ambience and function of nodes, improves interchange. If the park has only one bench, add another and plant some flowers. Assist the pizza restaurant to make the eating space more conducive to conversation. Clean the space around the shady tree. Assist the religious community and clubs in creating space that helps people to relax and enjoy each other's company. Create new nodal gathering places like a community plaza or garden.

5. Community Events
Every community event is an opportunity for effective interchange. Almost anything that gets people together provides the opportunity for genuine interchange to happen. They are high in interchange value. They include community celebrations, national holiday events, visiting speakers, funerals, sports, weddings, birthdays, school events or meetings, memorial events, town meetings, common planning events, village fiestas, children's parties, community theater, firesides, community forums, and picnics.

Begin working with events already on the calendar to make them better events. They can be improved and expanded. Beyond creating a good environmental atmosphere, the events may need better organization and facilitation. Look for invitations to offer to improve the events, especially those that require the community to make a decision together. Detailed planning and facilitation is critical. Involving as many people as possible in the planning and enabling of the events is extremely important.

6. Planning Events

The planning event is one of the best forms of interchange, especially in sessions where the community shares its common vision. Make business meetings more interesting with facilitation that ensures decisions are made. Serve refreshments after the meeting for informal interchange after the business is over. Planning events that invite the whole community to participate can be occasions to report to the community and engage them in planning the future. A community should have at least two community-wide planning events each year that involve all segments of the community.

7. Work Projects

The nature of work projects makes them great interchange events where the community comes together to do a task like cleaning the community streets. Always have a celebration after the work experience, reflecting on the event and praising the accomplishments and the people who made it possible.

8. Organizations

Both formal and informal organizations such as cooperatives, clubs, ball teams, and sewing bees, build long term relationships among people that can flow over into commitment to the community. The community makes possible the existence of the organization. Look for ways to create organizations that continue on their own. Competition between other communities is a strong builder of esprit-de-corps.

9. Shared Victory

A community can unite equally well around both great accomplishments and great strife; but in order to so, interchange has to be facilitated in a healing and inclusive manner. Victories and crises present opportunities for the community to become more closely united.

10. Indirect Communication

Indirect communication through community newspapers, bulletin boards, announcements, phone conversations, and yearly reports are valuable interchange; but they cannot replace face to face interchange.

D. IN THE ABSENCE OF INTERCHANGE

In communities where little or no interchange exists, more effort is needed to begin the formation of community. Events are needed to enable interchange, creating occasions for community residents to come together for whatever purpose – to appreciate one another and to learn to respect and trust each other. One may begin by forming a small group to work toward community formation through informal get-togethers like pot luck dinners. Community developers then find ways to enlarge the participation until the whole community has the option to participate. Not everyone will participate; but all should have the opportunity to do so.

One effective approach is to create a *common mission*. Take an issue facing the whole community that represents a *felt need* that the whole community is likely to be interested in solving. Then invite the entire community to a meeting to discuss the issue, create an action plan to deal with the problem, and get volunteers assigned to specific tasks to activate the plan. Examples of issues communities have focused on include: trash disposal; children dying from dysentery; absence of community services; and junk cluttering inner city community streets.

A community work day is one of the best ways to get to know others and build camaraderie. One's relation to work is very revealing about a person. Working alongside a person, one can tell a lot about that person's attitude toward life in general as well as toward work in particular.

E. THE LARGER INTERCHANGE

Eventually interchange will be required to relate the community to the larger society. In this way the local community assumes responsibility for the communities outside its boundaries and recognizes the interdependence communities have with one another. This interaction outside the community intensifies a community's identity and deepens the relationships within the community. The emphasis, however, focuses first on interchange within the community to build a sense of community. Community members then can self-consciously interact with other communities, state governments, the nation, and the globe.

CONCLUSION

To be a community people need to respect and trust each other, which requires interchange. It requires face to face interaction as well as all other forms of sharing. Interchange creates mutual respect and trust, creating a sense of being an integral, concrete part of a specific community. It nurtures the spirit of community and one's commitment to the community, integrating the community into a common human reality. Any time people get together around something they care about, there is interchange of knowing, doing and being.

II. AWAKENMENT

Toward Response-Ability

A. Levels of Awakenment

1. Expanded awareness
2. Becoming more comprehensive
3. Seeing in a new way
4. A paradigm shift
5. Exposure and conviction

B. Gifts of Awakening

1. Freedom to be authentic
2. Affirmation
3. Ability to be responsive and responsible
4. Quality of life
5. Self-esteem
6. Vibrant living
7. New possibilities

C. Guidelines for Community Awakening

1. Exposure
2. Gentle persuasion
3. Rude awakening
4. Conflict mediation
5. Careful contexts
6. Reflection

I once heard that the renowned philosopher Socrates classified people in two categories – pigs and persons. Pig people go through life unselfconscious, functionally unaware or uncaring of others or the civilizing process, focusing primarily upon themselves and their needs. Persons, on the other hand, are awake and attentive to their surroundings and sensitive to others. They are self-conscious and intentional about living their lives. They are grateful for life and careful to appreciate all of it. Person people are the ones who take responsibility for the formation of community.

Until we are aware of the realities of community issues and possible options, we are not able to be responsive to and for the community. Responsibility arises from an awareness that calls us to respond and shapes our ability to be responsive. At the heart of a responsible person is an awakened consciousness that makes response-ability an option. Our moral conscience is birthed in awakenings; it is a derivative of an enlightened awareness. The awakening of awareness jars loose avalanches of responsibility. Aldous Huxley in his book *Island*, suggested that society should have parrot-like birds that constantly announce, "Attention! Attention! Be awake! Stand at attention before the living of your life."

A. LEVELS OF AWAKENMENT

1. Expanded Awareness
Expanded awareness is added knowledge or information that expands our consciousness. It is learning something you did not know that 'fits in' with what you already know – new facts, new ideas, new theories, and new possibilities. It clarifies and confirms what one already knows and perceives to be true.

2. Becoming More Comprehensive
A deeper dimension of expanding awareness occurs when new awareness enables us to be more inclusive and comprehensive in our thinking and action. Expanded consciousness makes us more alive to the realities around us and more sensitive to the subtleties and nuances of the situation with which

we are dealing. We become more global in outlook and at the same time more connected to the local reality in and through the global context. Because one operates out of a larger context, with a more global perspective, one is more connected to life in general and the local situation in particular.

3. Seeing in a New Way

Seeing with new eyes or from a different position is another level of awakening. When you see things through the eyes of another person, as when you are expecting a visit from your mother-in-law, you begin to see the condition of your house in the way she is going to see it. It happens by seeing from a new point of reference or perspective, from a new position that gives a new viewpoint.

Reality can appear different when standing in a new place to look at the same thing. Things 'change' while staying the same. Sometimes it's like becoming aware of what you already know in a new or deeper way. It is a shift, a climate change. It is more than the sum of being more informed. It usually results in forming a new attitude toward what you already know and do.

The Montgomery, Alabama bus boycott launched a movement that awakened a nation to the dehumanizing effect of segregation upon the oppressor as well as the oppressed. It also awakened a people to the power of united action in securing equality for the black community. The awakenings eventually led to sweeping new civil rights legislation, voter registration, new political power for the black minority in the United States, and a nation sensitized to the injustices that existed and continue to exist as a nation. The awakening made the national government more responsive and responsible to its citizens.

4. A Paradigm Shift

A paradigm shift occurred when Copernicus saw that the earth was not the center of the universe as everyone assumed. When someone noted that the masts of the ships were the last to disappear as the ships sailed away, they must have wondered whether the earth was as flat as everyone thought. A paradigm shift alters one's model and perception of reality, one's concept of the way things 'really are.' It may result in a fundamentally different understanding about life and the value that one places on life and living. It may require new commitments to new demands.

A university student, working alongside of a local villager to dig a reservoir for the potable water project, found himself humbled by being 'out-worked' by a 57 year-old man. The experience awakened him to his false assumption that poor people are poor because they are lazy. He was moved, he said, to re-evaluate his intended vocation to be more responsive to the poor of the world.

At a community health fair the village residents were invited to look through a microscope to see things crawling around in the water they were drinking. They learned that this was what was causing the dysentery that was killing children on the average of one every month. It altered their image of reality. The awakening motivated the villagers to work hard for the next six months to get safe drinking water and sanitation facilities in the community.

5. Exposure and Conviction

Sometimes awakening jars us into seeing clearly what we have been refusing to see or to know about life in general or one's life in particular. It may reveal that one has been living in an illusion that has controlled one's thinking, feeling acting , as happened with the university student who assumed that people were poor because they were lazy. Or it may reveal that the community has been hiding from a truth about life and the awakening requires facing it squarely and coming to terms with it. This type of awakening exposes illusions and requires change. Being exposed and convicted, one is freed to deal with the revealed truth.

My friend John told me he did not think that he was a coward until the night he found himself in a life-threatening riot at which time he panicked and ran. When he became aware of his proclivity to panic and run when afraid, he had to face this new image of himself, accept it as true and what is more, affirm himself as that person (especially, if he was to continue to live in the dangerous place where he had chosen to serve). On the other side of acceptance and affirmation of his reality, he was then able, in the next threatening situation, while still frightened, to courageously stand firm and deal rationally with the situation. He was freed to deal with his cowardliness. Thus he was no longer a coward, or at least he became a courageous coward. He may still run, but not unthinkingly in cowardly panic. He was able to take a new relation to his proclivity to panic when frightened.

When we face our illusion, accept the reality, and affirm our condition and ourselves, we are given the freedom to choose to change our situations and ourselves. This is true for communities as well as individuals.

B. GIFTS OF AWAKENING

1. Freedom to be Authentic
John was given the opportunity to deal with his real self when the awakening event revealed to him his inclination to panic when threatened. Choosing to 'have' the being that he was, gave him his authentic real life. Choosing to love his 'real being' gave him the power to live authentically his actual life and then change it. When a truth is revealed to us, we have to both choose to have the true life that is revealed and choose to love it in order to authentically live our real life. Only living the actual, non-illusionary life is authentic living. It gives the freedom to grow, to change.

The turning point is decisional love. We have to say yes to the life we have before we can authentically live it. This is a decision to love our life and does not have anything to do, in the first instance, with feeling a certain way. Rather, it is the decision to choose to affirm the life we are given in its entirety. The alternative is to hide in an illusion or, being aware of the reality, pretend to be real while ignoring and hating the truth. Both responses are a negation of the truth, a refusal to have the real life: one to hide, the other to hate. Both deny us our authenticity. The negation of our actual life binds us to inauthentic living. For John it would have meant remaining the one who runs when afraid even while pretending otherwise.

2. Affirmation

Affirmation puts us in charge of living our lives. Only the person who chooses to love the life they have is free to change their life. If they pretend things are not the way they actually are, they are not going to be able to effectively influence what is and what is to be. People who hate their life diminish the possibility of changing their life. They may even reach a state of being unable to be aware of their actual real life condition. What is true for the individual is true for the community. If the community pretends it is something it is not, then it is not going to operate effectively or alter its conditions.

In choosing to relate to our given life as good, we acquire the freedom to self-consciously take charge of living our lives. The person who chooses to love the given life as revealed is freed to both live effectively the real life they have and change it if they so choose. An awakening offers this opportunity.

3. Being Responsive and Responsible

The depth function of awakening is that it enables one to assume responsibility for one's life and one's world. Awakenings call us to choose to be responsive, the first step in being responsible. Awakenings give us the means to be responsible, that is, to be 'able-to-respond' to an increasingly 'more true' reality. The sense of having a responsibility comes out of awakenings. The capacity to be responsible comes from accepting the awakenings and affirming the reality revealed therein.

4. Quality of Life

A Native American saying states that, "The quality of life is not measured by its length, but by the fullness with which we enter into each present moment." Every awakening offers a new chance to affirm life anew and stand self-consciously present to our lives. It intensifies our living and the appreciation of the wonder and value of being alive. We experience the profound value of life in general and our life in particular. We grow in selfhood and personal self-esteem increasing our capacity to appreciate life and living. Quality of life is enlivened in affirmed awakenings

5. Self-Esteem
Being responsible produces in us the sense of being a valuable part of the human race and a contributor to the advancement of humankind. We become part of the world-wide, history-long march toward something better: a more compassionate and kindly existence. We acquire the status of a mature adult in the eyes of the world. Being responsible relates us to others as a valued and helpful person, a valued part of the journey of the humanity.

6. Vibrant Living
Awakening creates in us a new appreciation of living and thus a capacity to enjoy life in gratitude and appreciation for all of life's gifts, large and small. D.H. Lawrence says it well, "Giving is still the truth about life. Even if it's a woman making a dumpling or a man a stool. If life goes into the pudding, good is the pudding, good is the stool; and we ripple with life through the days." Someone said it is like "having one's fist stuck fully into the belly of life." As life is intentionally expended, life flows back in as expanded energy; and we are vibrantly alive, able to more profoundly enjoy life and give of ourselves.

7. New Possibilities
New possibilities are revealed and created within the awakening process. Awakenings call us to make possibilities a reality, demanding that we live the fullness of our possibilities. We grow into responsible human beings through the experience of awakenings where we discover new reality and are given the opportunity to decide to affirm both the new reality and our life anew in its entirety. The sense of having a responsibility comes out of the response that is evoked. The capacity to be responsible comes from affirming the reality revealed.

In summary, awakening is the pathway to personal freedom and responsibility. It is the doorway to selfhood and to personal fulfillment. As the saying goes, "The truth will set you free." The task of the community formation team is to create opportunities for awakening to occur, to structure programs that make awakenings likely to happen, to encourage the individuals of the community to be open and welcoming of the surprise of awakening, and to facilitate the embracing of the new reality.

C. GUIDELINES FOR COMMUNITY AWAKENING

Merely living always provides awakening events, even when we do not seek them. However, one only has to be open to see and receive them. Many things expose us to awakenings that expand awareness: a crisis properly handled, a victory celebrated, a failure that is a learning experience, new information effectively presented, inspiring visitors, serious drama, a health fair, community planning, travel, recognition, visioning exercises, a courageous act, exchange programs, and readings – the list is endless. In fact, any event can become an awakening event for those who have eyes to see. All seven whistle actions double as powerful awakening agents, especially interchange, education and demonstration.

1. Exposure
Exposure is the first principle of awakening. You don't get the picture if you don't get the exposure. Although merely living exposes us to new awareness, the process can be intensified. More exposure creates more awakening. Exposure to:
- *Greatness* in the form of great persons, groups, achievements, ideas, events, movements, historical events, perspectives, and role models.
- *The 'other'* as in that which is different from us, is likely to break loose awakenings - different people, new experiences, other communities, travel in foreign countries.
- *Clear hard facts.* As far as possible have the facts straight and clear in all the efforts of exposure. Correct, 'hard' facts are important so the experience is based on clearly objective reality, not hearsay or obtuse, unclear information.
- *Logical sequence* is crucial, not only to have the correct information, but also to have a presentation that is clear, orderly and easy to grasp. Without this the experience can go off course.

2. Gentle Persuasion

Gentle persuasion is the preferred approach. Showering people with positive images of significance, possibility, and well-being floods the imagination and leads to being open to awakenings. Space is important for awakening by gentle persuasion. Our minds are constantly absorbing and processing messages that are stated or implied in our environment. If the environment is screaming that life is a worthwhile and orderly then we are going to be more likely to be open to the awakening dynamic that is latent in every event. One of the first things to do is mold an environment that will create an expectant spirit.

An inner city slum with vacant lots, boarded up buildings, dirty streets constantly announced to all who walked there that life is deterioration, powerlessness, and frustration. In the formation program it was urgently necessary to quickly alter the surroundings. "One day miracles" were held. Large pictures were painted on the walls of vacant buildings. The business district building fronts were painted in one workday. A playground was created in a prominent vacant lot using scrap from the community. Other signals that announced a new order were uniforms for the preschool children, community bulletin boards, street names, painting light posts and curbs, and planting trees on vacant lots.

Programs can bombard the community with images of value, possibility and hope. In the training to be a cooperative the village meetings always began with a listing of problems. During the discussion, the problems would be transformed to be perceived as windows of opportunity to a better future. The ending ritual of the meeting was, "We have no problems, only opportunities." A new attitude toward solving 'problems' was formed creating new openness to see possibility.

We see what we expect to see. If we can create the expectation of new possibility (an attitude of openness and hope in the future), we are better positioned to see and grasp new possibility when it arrives. If we are not anticipating something good to come, we will likely miss seeing it when it comes.

More often than not, it comes hidden in the mundane, every day living. We see what we are waiting and willing to see.

3. Rude Awakening

Rude awakening is sometimes necessary. Some times only a shock breaks the hold of dehumanizing attitudes, beliefs, and practices. Generally speaking, formulators of communities do not have to worry about shock treatment because life itself provides sufficient shocks to open people to look deeper in their lives to see the way life is and to discern the required response. More often than not, the facilitator's job is to help people appropriate the shocks given by life so that they can be dealt with creatively. Where it is necessary to initiate a shock treatment, the main guideline is to be sure the shock is coming out of love for the community and not resentment or hurt or some other negative motivations.

An 'over-againstness' is the least offensive and less dangerous shock treatment. This process is comprised of stating a position in a strong, authoritative, non-hostile manner. When someone or something presents a strong and clear presentation that authoritatively states that the truth is X rather than Y, then others have to make a decision to either agree or disagree and thus become aware of where they stand.

4. Conflict Mediation

Conflict mediation can be an awakening event. The first step is to get the conflicting parties in a neutral setting where the issues can be dealt with calmly. Secondly, begin not with the disagreement but with the points of common agreement to form a contextual framework in which to deal with the areas of disagreement or conflict. This can be a mutually desired future vision or a common set of operating values. Thirdly, let each one in turn present his/her position and reflect it back so there is no doubt by either party that both sides are being understood. Finally look for a third position that is better than either of the two conflicting positions to satisfy both parties. Don't let fear of conflict block decisive action to get the issue on the table and mediate. Conflict is bad only when it festers and grows and turns to hatred. Most people do not want to stay in a state of conflict, so are open to offers of mediation.

5. Careful Contexts

Careful contextualization can ease stressful awakenings. Much of what we see and how we experience a given situation depends on the context in which we are operating when we have the experience. The context shapes our interpretation of the experience.

I was greatly frustrated by driving in Venezuela. The traffic was so congested that I would have to wait at the intersection to a main road for a long time until I had a lengthy opening before moving into the traffic flow. Meanwhile, the horns blowing behind me did not help. Then I learned that the operating context of the Venezuelan drivers was that whoever can get out in front of another vehicle had the right of way, so one did not have to wait for a wide opening, a one-car opening worked just fine. The person driving behind expected the intrusions and willingly braked to permit the intruding car. With this new operating context, my driving became easier and safer because I knew to be prepared to brake and not to be frustrated by cars intruding in front of me; and I was able to get more quickly into the line of traffic and to my destinations.

Frustration is a result of expectations not met. We get angry, anxious and blocked when the expectations we have are not met. The context-expectation in which we operate greatly influences how we experience and respond to the experience of any given situation. Many times a situation can be experienced more positively if one has been given an adequate context to receive and appropriate some awakening news. A good context can make a difficult experience meaningful and thus easier to endure and participate in hard decisions creatively. An adequate context frees people to participate and gives them new eyes to see their situation in a new or more comprehensive way.

6. Reflection

Awakening experiences must be appropriated, which necessitates a reflective process to enable one to recognize, acknowledge, process and internalize new experiences. Reflection allows us to self-consciously experience our experiences. Reflection enables us to see the deeper significance of an event and to choose a self-conscious relationship to it. Reflection processes disclose the fear and fascination of living that we refer to as awe, making living an awesome experience, an experience of mysterious wonder. Sometimes we can be overwhelmed, confused or crushed by the weight of new awareness. Reflection mediates the difficult experiences.

A group of people on a global odyssey experienced parts of the world that they had only seen 'once removed' on television. They were shocked when children with no hands came to beg from them; but then they learned that their hands were cut off when they were babies so they would be more effective beggars. This was totally unacceptable. They saw inexplicable poverty, misery and inhumanity so blatant they were not able to absorb and deal with the horror of the experience. One participant expressed it, "I wish I did not know what I now know, because knowing it, I somehow feel responsible and can't do anything to help. Frankly. I really don't want the weight of knowing all this." The odyssey leaders provided a reflective process that allowed the group to assimilate the experience and take a self-conscious relationship to these new experiences. Without such an opportunity for reflection, the travelers would have tried to cope with what they had seen by retreating from this knowledge, only to have it appear in nightmares.

There are four fundamental reflection steps that cooperate with the natural functioning of the brain and the psyche in order to be fully aware of and to 'experience' our experiences. Reflection proceeds in this order to maximize the awareness of the experience and embrace the impact.

- **Objective description.** The first step is to describe as objectively as possible the object, person, event or happening. First articulate what was perceived as having happened as factually as possible without expressing one's emotional response or trying to interpret, evaluate or understand it. Disconnect your self and your emotions momentarily to state as factually as possible what was seen, touched, smelled, heard or tasted. State as objectively as possible who, what, when, how, how many, what time. To assist a group reflection in this first step, questions like the following are asked: *"What images do you recall? How many objects? What was the sequence of events? Who were the characters?"*

- **Interior impact discernment.** The second step is to describe the physical and emotional impact of the 'event' in order to clarify the impact on our interior being. This step focuses on what emotions were activated and what physical manifestations reveal the impact of the object of reflection: *"Where were you restless, nervous, or anxious? Where did you want to get up and move? How did it make you feel? What did you like or dislike? Who did you identify with in the drama? Where were you afraid or angry, bored, excited, anxious, fearful, fascinated, expectant, warm, uncomfortable, delighted, sleepy?"*
- **Interpretation.** The third step is to interpret, to think about what happened, and to ask what are the implications, meanings and significance of the experience. Describe what was going on in the event.. Questions of why, what for, how come, so what, and what does this mean assist this step: *"What caused this to happen? What is going on underneath the happening? What is important to note and what is not important about the object/event? What value does it have for us? What can we know or learn from the event? What is the significance and why is this significant?"*
- **Decisional choice.** The fourth step is to decide how to relate to the experience at this moment. Decide what the truth is for you. A good way to reflect on the decisional relationship is to think of a name to give to the experience because our relation to anything is disclosed in what we name it (e.g., s/he is a friend or enemy; the party was a blast or a washout, life is an adventure or a bore). The name you choose reveals your chosen relationship to the subject of reflection.

If you don't make a decision, you are left hanging, floating in relation to the awakening experience; and life passes you by without appropriating the experience. So make a decision, knowing you are free to make a new decision later on. Affirm or negate; believe or not believe, take a position, a stance in relation to the event in this moment. "What will you honor, or act upon, agree or disagree with? How will you act on the information or postpone action? What do you choose to believe about the experience? What is the life decision in relation to the awakening? What effect will you permit this to have on your life?"

This reflective four-step process can be incorporated in all group or individual reflections. It can be used in programs such as serious conversations, self evaluations and mediations. A conversation on a current news event is effective in deepening one's awareness and perception of the world. In news conversations it is good to decide (4th step) what you would do if you were the one responsible for dealing with the event under discussion (i.e., "If you were the U.S. president on 9/11 when terrorist planes struck the twin towers of New York City, what would be your response?").

Of course, every moment of living has the possibility to reveal the mystery and wonder of living and gives a more valid and comprehensive perception. So we need to regularly 'step back to take stock', to center ourselves so we can relate effectively to what is happening to us and experience the deepest value and importance of any part of our lives. To acknowledge awakening, affirm it and choose to live it.

CONCLUSION

The task then of community leaders is to structure programs that make awakenings to new awareness likely to happen, to create the opportunities for awakening to occur, and encourage the community to be open and welcoming to the surprise of awakenings.

III. DEMONSTRATION

Toward Courage and Hope

A. Demonstration Is ...
1. Like a light
2. Possibility taking visible form

B. Gifts of Demonstration
1. Renews faith in life
2. Restores faith in our potential
3. Releases courage
4. Uncovers hidden resources
5. Overcomes inertia
6. Provides determination
7. Converts cynics

C. Demonstration Guidelines
1. Visible
2. Fast and easy
3. Small is beautiful: think small and shout big
4. Felt need
5. Do common things in extraordinary ways
6. Address major contradiction
7. Highlight the victories
8. Involve as many as possible

What happens to a dream deferred?
Does it dry up like a raisin in the sun?
Or fester like a sore - And then run?
Does it stink like rotten meat?
Or crust and sugar over like a syrupy sweet?
Maybe it just sags like a heavy load.
Or does it explode?

If this poem of Langston Hughes[1] describes the experience of your community, then the vitality of your community and the people who call it home is at risk. For communities in this situation, demonstrations of possibility are a life and death matter.

The philosopher Ortega y Gasset said, "We anticipate our entire future, more or less clearly, at every moment." When the future we anticipate is so bleak or uncertain that we want to shut it off, we have reached a dark night of the soul. The Biblical proverb 29:18 states, "Where there is no vision, the people perish." Without a vision we continue in the morass of the present dysfunctions until there is no future worth having; and we cease to love the present we have. When we want nothing in the future, nothing is meaningful in the present save that which enables us to escape remembering we have a future.

When hope dies, the will to dream dies and along with it the courage to be, the belief in the goodness of life, the value of living, and the desire and will to struggle to make something better for our lives. Even the ability to simply enjoy the wonder of existence fades and hopelessness drains the joy of living; we become empty emotionally, going through the motions of living.

Where hopelessness exists, the malaise is dealt with by demonstrations of possibility that inspire hope in the future and courage for the present struggle. In one village project the sense of hopelessness was so pervasive that one would often see men sleeping off their alcoholic stupor in the streets in the early mornings. This phenomenon disappeared following a few visible

---

[1] *The Collected Poems of Langston Hughes*, Langston Hughes, Arnold Rampersad,1995, Vintage Classics.

victories that heralded the possibility of a new future. Where the malaise is not pervasive, demonstrations are not 'life and death' necessities. None the less, they are helpful in maintaining a lively morale and a vibrant motivation for working in the community.

A. DEMONSTRATION IS ...

1. Like a Light in a Field of Darkness

During World War II the civil defense presented demonstrations at the football stadiums by cutting all the lights and then having one person light a match. The effect was dramatic. It showed how powerful one tiny light can be to lead enemy aircraft to our door. A demonstration of possibility is like that small light. It can make a big and dramatic difference in a dark night of the community. A demonstration of possibility may be the flicker of light at the end of a tunnel that sparks the courage to continue the journey, releasing the energy to continue to put one foot in front of the other.

2. Possibility Taking Visible Form

Demonstration is hope incarnated. It is visible for all to see, observable possibility. It is concrete, specific, undeniable possibility. It is available for everyone to experience. It creates the awareness that something new is possible. Demonstration provides a peek into the future, a possible vision seen through the concrete manifestation of possibility. Showing what is possible is far more powerful than telling.

In a classic story showing the power of demonstration a lady was living as a guest in an Asian community where all the elderly people were stooped over with permanently bent backs. Their backs were bent because the elders were responsible for cleaning the streets which they did with short handled brooms, the use of which solidified a stooped posture as they grew less and less flexible. The lady used her long handle brooms purposely in the front of her house at times when she knew she would be seen. Then she invited some of the ladies to tea and left the broom visible on the porch for the ladies to see. She found a way to let it be known that these long handles were available to be harvested only a short distance from the village. Soon she noted that the men left on the water-buffalo in the direction of the long reeds. She moved away before the long handle brooms became accepted in the village. But some considerable time later, she received a beautifully written letter saying, "Thanks to you Lady our elderly no longer suffer with bent backs."

B. GIFTS OF DEMONSTRATION

Few things empower a community more than seeing new possibility take living form. The impact is always profound. It ushers in a fresh breeze of hope and anticipation. It opens people to see a better way. It gives them courage to risk change. It releases hidden and untapped resources in the community. This is especially true if people work together and experience their unified power in a common effort to make visible a new possibility. Large or small demonstrations are all miraculous in their impact. They are always dramatic and powerful, so they don't have to be big stupendous events.

Demonstration…

1. Renews Faith in Life
Demonstration of possibility inspires hope and faith in the future which in turn is an affirmation of the present. It renews our belief and trust in the fundamental value of life. We are enabled to trust in the benevolence of creation and the meaningfulness of existence. It enables us to see life as a journey, rather than a prescribed, predetermined, destination. It supports a sense of the mystery and wonder of living.

2. Restores Faith in Our Potential
When we believe a positive future is possible for everyone, we believe in our own potential, the power of one and the ability to make a difference. This faith can alter the basic attitude toward all of life.

3. Releases Courage
Seeing new possibility take shape in front of one's eyes releases one's courage

and willingness to risk change to realize a possible future. It fosters the willingness to be open to growth, which involves leaving the old and embracing the new, and having the courage to risk taking a chance on new beginnings.

4. Uncovers Hidden Resources

Seeing new possibility take living form releases hidden resources in the community. Hopelessness drains a person's energy even before any action begins. Hopefulness energizes the body. When a community begins to have hope, talents emerge that were hidden; and they are offered to the community. People begin to volunteer to do things where before they kept to themselves. People are able to work longer and learn faster when a hope-filled spirit invades their life. Hopefulness fills people with a desire to accomplish things.

5. Overcomes Inertia

A group of fourteen people concerned with renewal of community was given a bargain price on an unused school building covering a city block in an inner city slum. The buildings were a mess, having been unused for a long time. Cleaning was obviously going to be an overwhelming job. On the third day of cleaning inertia set in. Everyone was moving like snails. One leader read the situation and decided to take a small three by four meter area and make it a gorgeous site, creating a demonstration of what the whole place might look like when the cleaning and remodeling was complete. The members were invited there for refreshments. Seeing the possibility of the renewed space reinvigorated the team to return to the two-month long task of cleaning the whole city block of buildings. Refreshments each day in that small space maintained the spirit until the possibilities were evident elsewhere.

5. Provides Determination

A demonstration of possibility is like the flicker of light at the end of a tunnel that can spark the courage to continue the journey and release the energy to continue to put one foot in front of the other. Demonstrations can provide the determination to persevere and the motivation and strength to stand in the face of difficulties and adversity.

6. Converts Cynics

Cynics are usually people who care deeply but have never found an effective way to express their care. Demonstrations of effective care transform them.

In a Latin American village there was a man who was always known to say, "Nothing is going to change, why bother with trying." In the early weeks of formation the village community decided they wanted their name written on a hillside like they had seen in another village. Almost the whole village turned out to work on it. Old and young, male and female carried rocks up the hill, painted them with whitewash, and placed them to form the name of the village. It cost only a few pesos and was done in half a day. At the following celebration the local cynic was overheard saying, "Anything is possible when we work together."

C. DEMONSTRATION GUIDELINES

1. Visibility

The demonstration must be specific, observable and visible to all with little or no interpretation needed to perceive that it is a demonstration of possibility.

2. Fast and Easy (and cheap)

Look first for easy things that can be done quickly.

In a Latin American village the community had set aside a block for the community plaza, an important symbol for communities in Latin America. It was little more than an open space with a small shack-like pavilion and one bench. It was on the main road where mule trains and cars drove through the middle of the open space. In the first week of formation the villagers brought large rocks, which they painted and placed to define the edges of the plaza. This forced the cars to drive around the plaza in the space left for a road. Suddenly there was a plaza well defined and the villagers were happy and proud. Later more costly improvements were made for the plaza; but nothing rivaled the 'creation' of the plaza.

3. Small is Beautiful

Think small and shout big. Don't be afraid to do small demonstrations, because they too have big impact. They do not have to be huge events to be miraculous with magical effect. They can be a mini-park with one bench and flowers, regular garbage pick up, a sign on a hillside, public cans for trash with the communities name, a community bulletin board, new trees planted, a playground, or a model house.

4. Felt Need

Try to touch felt needs so residents will immediately respond to them, such as the status of having a plaza in the community or the introduction of something that immediately improves living conditions like a playground for children or access to information or transportation.

In a rural village the demonstration of a Lorain stove made a big difference in the lives of the women. The simple clay stove encloses the fire, creating a chimney that carries the smoke above nose and eye level. The stove supports cooking pots so that the heat from the fire passes directly against the pot bottoms significantly reducing the amount of fire wood that has to be collected. The stove sped up the cooking time because it was a more focused and hotter fire than the open fires the women were used to using. The children were healthier because it reduced smoke inhalation.

One small, low cost demonstration put the women of the village more in charge of their lives. Women who are used to making clay pots already have the skills needed to construct a clay stove. Another advantage of the Lorain stove is that it raises the pots up so the women don't have to stoop over. Our demonstration model was table-high. The women of West Africa however would have none of this raised-up stuff. They were adamant that women were supposed to stoop over. They did make Lorain stoves because of the reduced fuel use; but they just made them six inches high.

5. Do Common Things in Extraordinary Ways to Pack More Punch

One urban community decided to remove all the trash in the community in one day. The old cars left in the street and the worn out refrigerators on the back porches and all other junk was moved in one day to a vacant lot in the community. The pile was so large that it took the city four days with trucks and front-end loaders to remove the junk from the lot.

6. Address the Major Contradiction
As the formation develops and the few, major problems that cause the many problems are identified, begin to look for demonstrations that can touch the major contradictions. When you touch the major contradictions, the impact is increased. It might be things like safe drinking water, basic nutrition, or parasite infection - things that produce many other problems.

7. Highlight the Victories
When something is accomplished, take the opportunity to spin a story about the significance of the victory and recognize the workers who contributed to it. Milk the victories for all they are worth. Publish them in the community news or bulletin board to call the attention of everyone to the demonstration of possibility and deepen the awareness of the accomplishment and its significance.

8. Involve as Many as Possible
Involve as many individuals and groups as possible in creating the demonstration.

CONCLUSION

Every community needs to constantly renew its courage and faith in the future to fill itself with hopefulness, especially in communities where the dreams have been deferred too many times and the willingness to dream is dying. Restore the courage to be, to dream, to risk, to believe in the future and to love the present by enabling the community to create demonstrations of possibility.

IV. EDUCATION

Toward Effective Living

A. 21st Century Education Methods

1. Intellectual Methods
- Research
- Problem solving
- Model building
- Group thinking processes
- Planning methods
- Listening methods
- Communication methods

2. Social Methods
- Facilitation methods
- Decision-making processes
- Consensus building processes
- Negotiation methods
- Conflict resolution
- Team building methods
- Social graces
- Health and hygiene
- Celebration methods

3. Spirit Methods
- Mission statements
- Reflection processes
- Rehearsing our self-understanding
- A meditative council
- Contemplation exercises
- Tapping intuitive insights

B. Designing Community Education Programs

1. Functional education
2. Formal education
3. Information education
4. Contextual education

My neighbor tells of driving through Mexico where he observed miles and endless miles of apparently subsistence living. When he and his wife stopped for lunch at a restaurant on the edge of the city of Durango, he was surprised to see a lot of new cars and people in the restaurant dressed in the latest styles. He wondered what was going on there: How did this island of prosperity exist in the midst of the countryside through which he had just passed? He found the answer in Thomas Friedman's book, *The World is Flat*: "The jobs are going to go to where the best educated workforce is with the most competitive infrastructure and environment for creativity and supportive government. It is inevitable. And by definition those people will have the best standard of living."[1]

Durango's prosperity began years before with a decision by the elders of the city to provide excellent education for the children, beginning with the early grades and going up. Over the years as the youth became an educated workforce, they attracted industry that provided jobs, which in turn provided tax income that allowed the city to produce infrastructure and the quality of life that is now enjoyed. This island of prosperity can be traced back to a decision to insure an effective education for the children.

The most important resource of any community is the people and the greatest resource of each person is their intelligence. To have that resource developed to its fullest potential is a life and death matter for the future of individuals and the community. Everyone needs the best possible education that the village can provide. Each person deserves an equal opportunity

---

[1] Thomas Friedman, *The World is Flat*, 2006, page 323.

to avail themselves of education they need to realize their full potential. A functional education for everyone (male and female) is essential for a community; and every opportunity to go beyond functional education will add even more momentum to the life of the place.

Everyone wants to be effective, to be productive, to make a difference, and to live to their fullest potential. To be effective requires lifelong education, which is best realized in a 'learning community' that constantly updates its information and methods of operation. Our rapidly changing environment requires this constant updating.

Education feeds the mind, body and spirit as surely as the food that we put in our mouth, and therefore is a lifelong necessity. When individuals neglect intellectual exercise and nourishment, they lose intellectual muscle. The same is true for the 'community's brain'. The community that does not continue to grow in shared wisdom begins to decline. When a community is constantly learning together, through contextual, functional, informal and formal education, it becomes a better community for all and remains vibrantly alive and healthy.

The task of community formation is to create a learning community that includes educational opportunities for all.

A. 21ST CENTURY EDUCATION METHODS

Education in the 21st century focuses on methods and tools. There is too much information being generated each day for anyone to be the 'final authority' on any subject and guarantee what people need to know at any given time and place. The demand is to provide methods and tools so a person can find the latest up to date information or knowledge needed to do what s/he wishes to do and the intellectual skills to process the knowledge and implement the implied action. Educational programs include intellectual, social and spirit methods. Let me expand on each of those categories, since they are not necessarily phrases that commonly used.

1. Intellectual Methods

Intellectual methods enable gathering, organizing, analyzing and prioritizing information. They enable one to think clearly and profoundly to choose the best actions. Intellectual methods are needed in the areas of:

- **Research**: Finding, acquiring, organizing and interpreting data. We need to be able to put facts and other data into a rational gestalt that holds the deeper meaning of the data in a succinct and understandable form that makes logical sense and illuminates the unity of all the data.
- **Problem solving:** Becoming educated means learning how to take an issue or problem and resolve it. That means learning how to go to the heart of a problem: deciding how to approach a problem, how to define its various parts, and to discern the core issue among many issues. With a good diagnosis one can clearly define the goals and the benchmarks to measure the successful resolution of the problem. To resolve a problem we need to know how to think strategically to insure long range success, to think tactically for practical applicability, and to design implementation plans with a timeline of specific concrete actions for ninety days that will be launched tomorrow. Then we need methods to daily discern how to maneuver as we implement the action plan, adjusting to the unexpected or unknown things that are thrown in the path on the way to the solution
- **Model building:** Training people to build and test models.
- **Group thinking processes**: Wiring minds together to think together quickly and clearly about common issues. This includes how to brainstorm ideas and gestalt them quickly into a rational, cohesive pattern. Then we need to know how to push the ideas to illuminate the intuitive wisdom hidden in the brainstorm data and arrive at a common consensus.
- **Planning methods**: Envisioning a future, analyzing what is blocking the realization of that vision, and creating a clearly defined plan to enable the community to move through the blocks to reach the vision. Residents need to know how to create a viable plan and successfully implement it.
- **Listening methods:** Hearing what is being said, and not said, with a third ear if you please. It is tremendously affirming to be genuinely 'listened to' and understood by another person. Stepping into the shoes of another requires delicate intellectual skills to reflect back what is being said so the

talker is affirmed and actually comes to understand him/herself better by having had someone really listen.

- **Communication methods**: Talking and writing in a way that makes sense to others. We need the ability to communicate with a clarity and force that can be absorbed easily by others. We need presentation methods that are specific, logical, succinct, coherent, and imaginative in our presentations. We need to be able to place the data in a sequence that enables others to grasp, understand, and be convinced of the position. We need to be persuasive in communication, not only to be understood, but also to be convincing so positions and opinions are taken seriously. We need to know how to sell our ideas to others and to be able to present our ideas in a convincing and pleasing manner.

2. Social Methods

Social methods are about relating to each other and functioning together as a cohesive whole while maintaining the tension of individual integrity. They allow respect, trust, loyalty and faithfulness to those we like and also to those we dislike.

- **Facilitation methods**: These enable us to run a meeting that gets something accomplished. They enable us to tap into the corporate wisdom with workshop methodologies that include brainstorming, forming a gestalt, interpretation, and then moving towards consensus.
- **Decision-making processes**: When a consensus does not exist, decision methods help us to decide together in a way that honors everyone's wisdom while maintaining a creative tension between individual and group wisdom.
- **Consensus-building processes**: These allow a group to journey step-by-step to form a general consensus that everyone agrees to accept and act upon, even though it may not be the first choice for everyone. The consensus maintains forward momentum for the group.
- **Negotiation methods**: These enable people to arrive at a win-win solution to issues that could otherwise divide them. These methods often help a group to find a third alternative beyond conflicting positions.
- **Conflict resolution**: Resolving conflict is similar to negotiation but starts from postures of hostility, and requires slightly different methods.

- **Team building methods:** These methods form cohesive, mission-oriented teams who work together on projects in a highly productive manner. They build a unity of loyalty to both the mission and to each other. They enable us to do the job and sustain each other in the mission at the same time. The processes include how to set roles, functions, lines of authority, and assignment. They involve methods of accountability and forgiveness. They keep the team focused in the midst of outside pressures and temptations.
- **Social graces:** Mastering a minimum of social graces always comes in handy so one can present oneself and one's assets in a more effective way.
- **Health and hygiene:** Some communities need education programs on health and sanitation methods that are essential to insure the energy to engage in community formation (e.g., how to eat right, to care for one's body, to care for babies and the elderly, to avoid parasites or treat them).
- **Celebration methods:** Celebration methods help community residents play together, enjoy each other's company and to affirm one other.

3. Spirit Methods

Spirit methods provide profound motivation; they instill the courage to be fully engaged, to risk exposure and to change. They mold discipline that provides the power to do what we decide to do, to keep our promises to others and to ourselves. Spirit methods clarify the values that define for us who we want to be. They create the interior resources that enable us to continue when the journey gets long and difficult. They enable us to maintain focus and commitment in the midst of distraction and to overcome disappointments and setbacks. They help us avoid burnout, keeping us vibrant. Spirit methods include:

- **Mission statements:** Written mission statements define the one thing that our life is to be about in our work and play. They unify the thrust of our lives, enabling us to get clear on who we want to be and what we want to do with our lives. They clarify the ultimate reference points for decisions. "Purity of heart is to will one thing," wrote Soren Kierkegaard. Getting clear on where we stand puts all our commitments in balance.

- **Reflection processes:** Reflection allows us to disengage, detach ourselves, and get perspective. It permits us to step back and see our prejudices or biases, our strengths and weaknesses, our options, possibilities and limitations. It helps us to manage anger, frustration, disappointments, and danger. It enables us to maintain an affirmative posture toward life. By rehearsing our self-understanding through symbols, stories, rituals and songs, we can remind ourselves of our decisions and commitments, which keep us steadfast in our engagement and obedient to our vision and values.
- **A meditative council:** We all have in our memory the people who have shaped our consciousness and values. When these colleagues are remembered, they guide our deciding and acting. They can be objectified and thereby used more effectively to guide our thinking and acting and free us from negativity.
- **Contemplation exercises:** Contemplation places us before the wonder, mystery and glory of the universe, the marvel of self-consciousness, the wonder and awe of living. Learning how to appreciate and love the life we have is an important dynamic of our lives. Teaching us how to contemplate daily is a critical task of education.
- **Tapping intuitive insights:** Exploring intuitions allow us to know what we know, which is always more than we know that we know. It provides holistic knowledge beyond our ability to rationalize or explain.

Intellectual, social and spirit methods are separated only to delineate the various dimensions. They are in fact inseparably one reality, one educational process. In all our thinking we need to learn how to be inclusive, how to honor the past wisdom but not be bound by it, how to be open to futuristic new possibilities but not sell our soul to it, and how to be self-consciously intentional in all we do. Education helps us to do and be these things.

B. DESIGNING COMMUNITY EDUCATION PROGRAMS

Our education is not complete until theories are applied to the practicality of daily living. "Action removes the doubt that theory cannot solve," said Chinese philosopher Tehyi Hsieh. Jean-Paul Sartre points out that we never fully know the reality of a situation until we begin to act to influence or change it. We get educated when we combine our knowing with doing and our being is manifested in vibrant living. Good education grounds us in the stuff of life, not in abstractions.

It is also true that education that is done for its own sake without regard for any practical usefulness has an important place in educational structures. This non-practical dimension allows the spirit to soar and the mind to break out of its boundaries. It releases creativity. It is done for the joy of knowing, for delighting in knowing, following curiosity, being there in the now. It indulges in the joy of learning, the pleasure of knowing found in arts, games, and puzzles.

1. Functional Education

Felt need is always a clue to where to begin anything. For education that usually means functional education. Obviously the need depends on the level of the educational development in the community. Some communities need very basic programs; more developed communities may need things like computer training for the elder generation. It depends on what resources are readily available and how quickly something can begin. Some examples of functional education might include the following 'how tos': make meals more enjoyable and nourishing, call for help in emergency, know where help is available, get around the city by reading a map, irrigate crops, make bread, build a clay stove, insure safe drinking water, dance, form a cooperative, and recognize health issues.

Almost all communities can use training in how to: create and carry out an action plan, manage a project to achieve desired goals, research information on specific problems, structure time to get done what needs to be done, and to husband resources, to manage them and maximize their value. Other effective places to begin include job retraining and how to begin an industry.

Basic information that all community members need to know may include:
  • Who is in the community?

- How many people are there?
- Who are the leaders?
- What are the power relationships?
- What services are available?
- What are the geographical boundaries?
- What are the rights, privileges and responsibilities of being a member of the community?
- What are the laws and regulations governing the community on local, state and federal, levels?
- How does the community operate?
- What are the societal traditions, the local customs and taboos that define the expectations of the community?

In villages where many people cannot read or write, providing a literacy class is a great place to begin to release hope for a better future. Materials and personnel for literacy training are often readily available nationally. One only has to invite the teachers to the community and assist them to begin the program. The glow in the face of a sixty-year-old man, who learns to read and sign his name, is a sight to behold and a force in the community for progress.

The horror of going through life unable to read came home to me in Hong Kong when I was separated from my host and lost in the heart of the city. Unable to speak a single word or read a street sign or talk with anyone was both frustrating and scary. In some situations it could be dangerous and life threatening.

2. Formal Education
Community formation always needs formal structures of education (e.g., preschool, primary and secondary schools, university and continuing adult education programs). Proficiency in reading, writing and arithmetic are always a goal of community development. It may take years to get the full complement of formal education established; however, formal training can begin immediately in one form or another.

Here is an example that drove home for me the crucial role of formal basic education in community development. I was surprised when a community meeting terminated abruptly while focusing on a subject in which all were very interested. I discovered that it broke up because the participants were at a point of deciding to buy or not to buy and could not continue until a villager was present who could do the math necessary to make the decision. He was gone from the village until the evening. Formal education is not a luxury. It is essential to life, a necessity for effective living.

Starting a preschool has multiple results beyond beginning formal education. It creates hope in the future for the parents who sense that their children may have a better chance then they had. It releases the women of the community to work in the community as well as tend to their family's needs. It can also be a learning and training experience for the parents, teachers and future leaders. Preschools can be launched with simply one teacher and parent volunteers.

3. Informal Education
Formal education can be supplemented by informal education that occurs in conferences, travel, short courses, home study, technical and training, health fairs, and nutrition courses. Valuable education is often accomplished informally during various community activities such as starting a preschool, researching for better irrigation, studying zoning regulations, forming a cooperative, raising funds for the community, initiating a community celebration, performing in a community theater, and attending community orientation sessions where people learn about being part of the community and the responsibilities of community membership.

4. Contextual Education
Society operates out of a 'common sense' understanding of 'what is what', what is real. This common sense is an expression of the science of the times that all assume is the way life is. The common sense understanding of reality guides our perception of reality and thus guides our thinking, deciding, acting and feeling. It indicates what is appropriate and inappropriate, what

works and does not work. It is a major part of the operating context out of which we decide and act. A wartime context makes sense out of very different things than a peacetime context of plenty.

In order to understand the influences that are impacting their lives and how to operate effectively, it is important for the community to have a 'common sense' orientation of the world that jives with the 'world view' of the rest of society or at least understand how they differ, and make adjustments to operate effectively in the larger society. If the larger society is operating out of one context and the community another, then there are problems. If the community is 'out of sync' with the rest of the society, it may be headed for a breakdown of fundamental relationships. It is especially conflicting for the youth who experience one understanding of reality at school that conflict with the image of reality at home.

If one is operating out of a past worldview, one loses effectiveness in operating in today's world to get things done, especially in relationships with other people. When one's common sense understanding is different from the larger society, one tends to feel sane while feeling the rest of the world is insane. This produces a withdrawal and an animosity toward the world in general. It is very difficult for people to alter their perception of reality so any change needs careful and delicate attention in the education arena.

CONCLUSION

People are the most important resource of any community and the human brain is the greatest resource of the individual. To have that resource developed to its fullest potential is a defining factor for the future of the community and for each individual's personal future. Everyone needs the best possible educational programs. Every member of the community deserves an equal opportunity to avail themselves of the education they need to realize their own full potential.

V. STORYTELLING

Toward Meaningful Identity

A. Community Storying is ...

B. The Function of Story

1. Fulfills
2. Animates and motivates
3. Guides
4. Creates 'a people'
5. Identifies

C. Creating Stories

1. Birthing
2. Appreciation and affirmation
3. Consensus
4. Honor the past
5. Attack the victim image
6. History-long and worldwide
7. Symbol

D. Specific Actions Contributing to Birthing a Story

1. The arts
2. Float balloons
3. Community workshops
4. Community planning events
5. Rehearse the history
6. Cross-fertilization
7. Crisis events
8. Tell and retell the story

In one way or another, we tell stories about who we are and why we do what we do, and the acts plus the story gives meaning to our lives. Stories define our self-understanding of who we are and what we do and why we do it.

When three brick masons were asked, "What are you doing?", the first one replied, "As you can see, I am laying bricks." The second answered, "I am earning ten dollars an hour." The third responded, "I am building a house for the Johnson family." Each man told a true story. Which man has the more significant and satisfying work? Among the workers on an assembly line making seatbelts, there were some just getting through the day and some earning a living; but one told himself that he was saving lives. The story we tell ourselves about our action defines our self-understanding of what we are doing with the expenditure of our lives.

Hitler's story proclaimed that the Aryan race was the superior race on the planet and that ended in tragedy for the world and for himself. The fathers of the American Revolution penned a story that announced that all men are created equal with the inalienable right to life, liberty and the pursuit of happiness, and the right to self-government. That story also got them in trouble; but it created a better future than the superior race story. Different stories lead to different actions. We choose our story; and our story creates our future.

Imagine that you are the CEO of a business that lost a lot of money due to mistakes made by a team of four people. You have decided to close that operation but keep one person to fill out a team on a different operation. In an exit interview you ask each why such a mistake was made. The first says, "I am not sure why I did what I did; I guess my colleagues gave me incorrect information." The second says, "I had no other choice; the circumstances required the decisions we made." The third says, "My spouse is always putting pressure on me to earn more money; and it caused me to take unnecessary risks." The last says, "I made a bad call. I am fully responsible. I intend to learn from the mistake." Which one of the four stories would you keep to place in the new team? We are the story we tell about out actions. Our stories illuminate who we have chosen to be; and then the stories assist in creating who we become.

Edison's experiments to invent the electric light were many, and at one moment his assistant proclaimed in frustration that they had failed for umpteen times. Edison's response was, "No, we have not failed; we now know umpteen different ways that it does not work." Same events, different story, different perspective, different motivation.

In one urban community there was a seventeen-storey building referred to by all as 'the old folks home.' This should have been a rich resource for community formation because there were a lot of retired human beings with time on their hands. But very little interest was shown for working in the community. Looking beneath the inertia, the operating story went something like, "We have been put aside by society to wait for death to take us. We are unwanted and useless to the rest of society." A new story was suggested, "Elders of society preserve the wisdom of the past that we all need to be effective and creative in solving the issues of the present and future. They are the depository of society's wisdom." When the new story took hold, the 'old folks' became 'the elders' and began to move. Some were instrumental in forming the community security watch in the somewhat dangerous neighborhood where the building was located. Others became teachers in the ethnic heritage course for the local preschool and in schools in neighboring communities. Some joined in the community planning for the future of the community. They became a vital force in the community.

The stories we tell about 'who we are' and 'what we do' create and sustain our awareness of the values we hold and how we value ourselves. That awareness shapes our perception of life and ourselves in general. Our perception shapes all of our feeling, thinking, deciding and acting. A community becomes the story that the residents choose to tell about themselves. It defines the quality of the community and guides its creation, forming the 'heart' of the community.

A. COMMUNITY STORYING IS

… appreciating the wonder and glory that is one's life and one's community

… telling the deep, poetic truth about life and the community where one resides

… illuminating the significance of the community to itself and to the world

… artfully embodying one's self-understanding about life, the values, concerns, hopes, dreams aspirations and intents of a person or a community

… proclaiming the gifts that the community brings to the civilizing process of the planet

… delineating the common values and assumptions that guide community consensus

… bringing self-consciousness to ultimate concerns out of which a community can operate and derive its basic self-understanding

… disclosing a community's posture toward life

… enabling people to become self-consciously 'a people' with a historical awareness

… defining a unique identity for the community

… revealing the meaning of the relationships that make up the community.

… inventing a common purpose for being

… turning matter into spirit.

A vital community always births a unique and meaningful identity. This primarily involves telling a story about what is important and uniquely meaningful about one's particular community—its gifts, its value, its contribution to the creation of civilization. It is creating a sacred history, a history that honors the expended lives that created the community.

B. THE FUNCTION OF STORY

1. Fulfills
Story illuminates a reason for being. It defines the common purpose of a community that makes the events of our lives a meaningful journey together

and imparts a fullness of life that comes from living in a community infused with meaning and purpose. A journey of meaning deepens the relationships between people, transmuting the stress that arises in living together into significant struggle. It makes living and working in the community meaningful and fulfilling.

2. Animates and Motivates

The common story animates the community by embodying the ideals, values and beliefs, goals, desires and intentions into a lively, artful story, giving life and vitality to the common self-understanding. It energizes a community. The story enables the community to be true to itself, to live up to its story. A good story releases a flood of motivation and a sense of direction and purpose.

3. Guides

A common story forms a consensus about the defining principles of the community that guides the decisions and actions. In times of stress the story calls us back to the fundamental values upon which the relationships are built and points us toward the future envisioned in the story. The story enables self-conscious awareness of who we wish to be and helps us to choose to be it.

4. Creates 'A People'

A story creates an awareness of being a unique body of people with historical existence and continuity, a historical entity in and of itself, a self-consciously unique entity within the historical process. The story makes us self-consciously aware of having a historical identity. It gives a sense of participating in a historical process as a unique body of people in the flow of history. It makes of the many 'a people'.

5. Identifies

The story tells us what it means to be the particular body of people that we are, and identifies who we are as a historical entity both for the outside world and us. It makes being a community historically real and thus satisfying.

The following are a number of stories that have shaped the creation of communities.

There was no U.S.A. and then an event called 'a tea party' led to a series of events later named a revolutionary war. A story was told about the right to independent self government and the equal right of all to life, liberty and the pursuit of happiness. Out of those events and story a self-conscious body of people was born into historical existence that eventually came to be known as the United States of America. Events without a story go nowhere. The King of England's self story was that it was a rebellion to be put down, but he lost out to the story that it was a revolution for the creation of a new people.

American women's right to vote was born out of the expenditure of courageous women who proclaimed the story that it is "the natural right of women to govern themselves in choosing their representatives; and the right to vote is the defining feature of full citizenship." Enfranchisement of women took many decades to realize because the male electorate (who made the laws) had a strong story that said women are dependent on men and subordinate to them, and could not be trusted to exercise independent thought necessary for choosing political leaders, nor were they "suited by temperament or circumstance to vote." It took from 1600 to 1910 to persuade the male electorate (and some women) of the truer story that called into historical existence 'a people' called the National American Woman Suffrage Association (NAWSA). The story finally took hold in five states in 1910 when Carrie Chapman won the right for women to vote in Wyoming, Utah, Idaho, Colorado, and Washington.

Here is a religious story. The governing model of the Roman Empire said that all non-citizens were mandated to abandon any local identity and accept the godship of Caesar as their operating reality. For persons who were not born into Roman citizenship, they were 'no people.' Then there was the event called Jesus. The story was told that he was the Christ, meaning the anointed one of an invisible God. That story gave birth to a self-identified body of people called Christians. As the story grew and mutated, new stories created many different self-conscious bodies of people with different Christian names. Every religion has its defining story.

Military bodies all have a story that defines their self-understanding and distinguishes them from other military units. The story of the U.S. Marines Corps is that they are the first and the best on land, sea and air from the halls of Montezuma to the shores of Tripoli, enabling them to stand tall.

The Boy Scouts have a twelve-point story that says a scout is honest, brave, loyal, kind, trustworthy, and courteous. When a boy buys into the story, he becomes at that moment self-consciously a scout and part of a historical body called Boy Scouts.

Mexican revolutionaries did not exist before 1910 when a man named Madero published the story that Mexicans had the right to elect their president and the right (and responsibility) to revolt against thirty years of dictator control if not given that right. That story birthed 'a people' called Mexican revolutionaries. Poncho Villa was a small-time butcher and a cattle-rustling bandito when Madero's story baptized him with new meaning. Villa was transformed into a fierce fighting machine and a revolutionary hero by the story that gave new and superior reason for doing what he was good at doing. The story made of him a new man. When he lost his story, he degenerated into a mad tyrant.

Historical bodies of people, be they monks, football teams, hippies, or corporations, all have their story that defines who they are and make sense out of what they are doing. Their stories communicate what it means to be an IBM employee, an American, a Russian, a Jew, a Muslim, a Christian, a Rotarian, a Harvard graduate, or a Yankee fan. Without a story we experience ourselves as 'no people,' homeless as a motherless child. Story is the key to identity.

The Marshall Islanders in the middle of the Pacific Ocean were eating fish out of imported tin cans. They had lost their heritage of being seafaring people who crossed the great ocean in canoes. It seemed that they had adopted the story that they were "the people found by the Englishman" who happened by and drew a map. Research uncovered the ancient 'stick-maps' that the ancestors had used to navigate the vast ocean in canoe-like vessels where navigation was based on the sounds that the water made on the side of the canoe indicating turning points on the stick maps. Stories of the courageous crossings were recovered. The sense of being a people of the sea returned. A new spirit emerged from the awareness of whom they had been and could become. The stories of the historic journeys of their ancestors captured for them a new sense of their value in the world. Soon they began once again to harvest the gifts of the sea and sing new songs.

> Sailing their ships upon the water,
> into a future in the blue,
> Strong men and women rode the currents,
> moved by a power they knew,
> *Ralik, Ratak, Ralik Ratak,*
> brave people born of the sea
> Once more we walk down to the shoreline,
> asking the waves which way to go,
> Dreams of a life once far beyond us,
> dreams of a future we know.

A story makes of the many one reality, a unity based on a deep kinship of common understandings about what is important and of value to the community. It reflects a consensus about the desires and intentions of the community that helps to weld the community into a solid whole.

C. CREATING STORIES

1. Birthing

Creating a new story is a birthing process. As in all births it is rarely easy going. It is a job for midwives and pregnant beings (male and female). A new story cannot be offered up on a platter for the community to accept. It cannot be imposed nor simply given. It can only be born out of the expenditure of the community. It does not happen overnight. It must be born and grow and mature and then be reborn once again. We sew the seeds and see what grows, matures and is transmitted into reality for each generation, "once and forever and ever again."

2. Appreciation and Affirmation

Appreciation and affirmation are the generating forces of the creative process, the start-up dynamic and main ingredients of the birthing. They are the glasses that enable us to see, the wellspring of inspiration, the 'where with all' of creation, the ground to stand on where all is possible for the imagination. This is the foundation for knowing, doing and being. Do whatever is necessary to bring to full awareness the community's gifts and value. Look for opportunities to appreciate and spell out the wonder and awe of being this community. What are the benefits the community has for residents and the larger community? What is great about being this community, in this location, in this time in history, its advantages, possibilities, and gifts? Sing the praises of the community at every opportunity. Promote a positive attitude of knowing and accepting one's situation and affirming it to release the interior freedom to imagine possibility beyond the present moment.

3. Consensus

A consensus process is the only way to birth symbols. Majority does not rule here. A 'one person one vote' majority cannot vote effective symbols into existence. The whole body of people must adopt the story as their baby. The story belongs to everyone in the community or it is not the community story. It cannot be imposed. At every opportunity practice a process of consensus, using majority vote only as last resort.

4. Honor the Past

Expended life makes a place sacred, the same as those who died there make a battlefield sacred. The more life that has been expended in a place, the more sacred the space becomes when expenditure is honored. One way to honor the past is to maintain the awareness that we always build on the lives of those who have gone before even if we do not know them. It is part of the appreciation of the life and place one is living. Research the history of the community and honor it. Knowing the past helps in discerning the unique gifts to give meaning to the present.

5. Attack the Victim Image

The victim image is a self-story of insignificance and powerlessness. It is always there when a community is poorly developed. It blocks the community from effective development. The victim image usually discloses itself in the early days of formation. Evolving a story of significance that cuts over against the victim image is the best way to alter this negative force in the community.

In a village in Latin America the 'patron image' emerged when the first planning session came to the point of deciding how to resolve the contradictions blocking the desired future. Irrigation was high on the vision priorities. The question was asked, "How are we to go about getting the desired irrigation equipment for the crops?" The first action proposed by the villagers was to go visit the president of the nation and ask him to provide it. When asked, "What is another action that might be taken?" the second suggestion was to write a letter to the president. They had no perception that one could get what one needed without asking the boss (patron) to provide it. Their self story was that they were powerless to alter their condition without help of the patron. With that self story they saw themselves as powerless, and thus unable to assume responsibility for realizing their desired goals.

The image pervaded the country. A CEO of a multinational corporation who became a friend of the project, often commented how he had to make all the decisions in the company, even decisions like where to place the table for the new coffee machine. No one was willing to assume the responsibility. "Let the jefe decide, it's safer that way" was the cultural norm for the whole society.

The best way to attack such de-motivating images is to tell a new story. A way to begin a new village story was found in the name of the village. It was named after a beautiful tree that was considered to be "good wood" because it was excellent for making furniture. A photograph of the tree was placed on a large poster with the name of the village and the caption "La Gente de Buena Madera" ("The People of Good Wood"). Each householder welcomed a poster and put it on their walls of stick, mud, or block. The people began to think of themselves in a new light, as good wood, like their name. The difference was noted and remarked upon by visitors from the neighboring community. It began a new story about how this village would pioneer an irrigation system on behalf of the nation. They eventually got a state of the art irrigation system, resulting in the average annual income of the farmers increasing ten times. The village became a site for visits from other communities and other nations.

In an inner city community the victim image was traced to the story people told themselves about the period of slavery as being a time of cowardly capitulation to superior forces. The community residents considered themselves inferior because they were descendants of slaves and thus not first-class citizens worthy of the development and resources available to others. It was necessary to retell the story of slavery: to see that period not as a capitulation to superior races but as a time of creative and courageous endurance that spread the gifts of black vitality across the world.

Until stories of low self-esteem, powerlessness and inferiority are changed, no lasting change is likely to be realized in the communities. Until the village decided they could resolve their own problems, until the retired community decided they were worthy and useful to society and their community, until the black residents decided being descendants of slaves was a rich heritage and not a shameful past, little else could be accomplished by whatever action was taken.

I have witnessed urban renewal housing developments return to slum dwellings in a little more than a year because there was no alteration in the sense of self-worth. So the new houses once again became slum dwellings, reflecting the interior self-story in which the residents were trapped. All of us make of our exterior world a reflection of our interior world. The only effective way to attack such de-motivating images is to tell a new story, by words, and deeds and inspiration. The alteration of the victim image is a matter of telling a truer story of significance and possibility.

6. History-Long and Worldwide

People may give some of their time to a project but they will not give themselves unless they grasp that their involvement is worthy of their unique, unrepeatable and mysteriously sacred life. Thus the community story must have worldwide, history-long significance to command the full respect of the residents. We human beings give ourselves to nothing less. Sensitive and aware people do not want to expend their lives in 'small time', 'small space' living. We all want to be a part of the whole because therein lies fulfillment. Only a story can provide wholeness. To inspire commitment from the members of the community, the story must enable them to grasp the significance of who they are, and what they are doing for the whole world and all of history.

7. Symbol

The story becomes part of the symbol system of the community that embodies the hopes, dreams and values of the community. We decide who we want to be and then put before us a symbol of that aspiration. The symbol calls to us and enables us to become what we aspire to be. The symbol system is the keeper of the conscience and the molder of the integrity of the community. Symbols point to a reality and enable us to participate in that reality. Witness the power of the song that became part of the story of the civil right movement, "We shall overcome someday."

D. SPECIFIC ACTIONS CONTRIBUTING TO BIRTHING A STORY

1. The Arts

All of the arts can be helpful in story telling. They get the juices flowing and give expression to the interior being of the community. The story elements may well emerge from work in the arts. Role-playing, writing, singing, song writing, dancing, poetry creation, drama, and acting - they all tap into the creative powers of people. Photography is a good place to begin. Get pictures of the community that have meaning for the community. Space images have power because they carry the memory of expended human life. Photos of the community and its people can illuminate the beauty and value of the community. They require one to stop and think of what they have seen through the artist's eyes. Poetry and songwriting is another good way to begin story creation. The community can use familiar tunes and create new poetry to go with the tunes that express their thoughts and feelings about the community. In one community the march from the opera Aida was the music the village had adopted for the village queen coronation during the yearly festival and so was an ideal tune to borrow and use for singing about the village.

2. Float Balloons

Test out new ideas in a way that allows you to pull them back or adjust them if they don't seem to resonate with the local community. An image for this sort of testing is to 'float balloons'. Present ideas and models for action in a small setting or in a group where exchange will happen easily to see if they take hold. Experiment with stories and images of significance. The community may adopt the stories or they may get shot down or simply ignored. Look constantly for new images and concepts that capture the imagination of the community. Try out things and see if the expression strikes a cord. But be willing to discard your creativity if it does not grab the attention of the community. If something does capture the imagination of the community, look for a way to develop the theme or concept or emotion. If the balloon stays afloat, then it may become part of the story.

3. Community Workshops

Community workshops can explore ideas and images for the story by brainstorming the images and then organizing them in a way that clarifies the common community understandings. Workshops can be about the dreams, common values, plans, gifts and blessings of the community, advantages, and vulnerabilities.

4. Community Planning Events

These are times for discerning the common story, especially in the workshops that envision the desired future that they are planning. Visioning and re-visioning is one of the best places to release the growth of story. The desired future is a reflection of the existing story operating in the community. Planning the strategy and tactics may reveal where and how the story is needed to empower the implementation of the plan.

5. Rehearse the History

Rehearse the history of the community and its individual members for all to be aware of the expenditure of valuable lives that brought the community to this moment in history. Naming streets can contribute to remembering the history. A chart of the history or a written account is helpful. But most powerful is the telling of the story of the history in public forums.

6. Cross-Fertilization

This occurs through interchange with other communities or individuals where the images and values of the community are contrasted with other values to clarify or augment the images of significance.

7. Crisis Events

Crisis events can be galvanizing events that clarify the community's beliefs and values and thus contribute to the forceful articulation of a more profound story.

8. Tell and Retell the Story

Tell and retell the story and retell it again. Telling the story develops the story like a fish story that increases in size with each telling. Put the story into rituals, songs, poems, and pictures. Tell it over and over so it grows, matures, and becomes ingrained in everyone's mind. Retell it until it becomes the story for everyone about life in the community. And then tell it again as it mutates into a clearer and more profound story. Put the story to music and sing it.

CONCLUSION

We human beings always tell ourselves a story about our lives and the events that impinge upon our lives. The events plus the story illuminate the significance of our lives, to us and to the world.

The birthing of a new or improved story, about the significance of the community (seeing who they are and can become), is probably the most important formation tool we have. When people are able to tell themselves a more adequate story, their lives are enriched, their self-esteem is enhanced, and their actions have meaning and significance beyond their individual lives. Stories tell us 'who we are'; they create and sustain our awareness of value and significance. This awareness shapes our perception of life and of ourselves. Our perception shapes all our feeling, thinking, deciding and acting.

If you can do only one thing to form community, tell stories. A community leader begins immediately, and continues forever, to enable the community to tell a more adequate story about being a part of the community. Let all the actions, meetings, and programs support the creation and telling of a new or better story about the significance of the community. Let everything contribute to a story that says that life is good as it is given, the past is approved, the future is open, anything is possible, and our lives are significant and valuable just as they are. We can take charge of living the lives we have, right now.

Toward Commitment

A. Direct Action is …

B. Benefits of Direct Action Care

1. Expands commitment
2. Releases 'Those Who Care'
3. Discloses hidden realities
4. Heals the community through acts of caring

C. Managing Direct Action

1. Genuine involvement
2. Specific, achievable and measurable
3. Pick winners
4. Felt need
5. Involvement
6. Celebrate the action
7. Engagement
8. Work projects

A family bought a plot of land near a beautiful beach intending to build a home, but vacillated about when to begin construction. Three years passed. Then one visit, with some extra time on their hands, they decided to protect their property with a fence, which they installed with their own hands and a little help. Then they decided they might as well plant some flowers and trees since the fence protected it. The plantings grew to one hundred plants which then required a watering system for the dry season to hold the plants until the rains came. Having done this much, they set a time to begin constructing their home. The small direct action of care given to the land made it easier to commit to the big step. The land took on new, deeper, personal value to them. Commitment grows out of direct action involvement. Action removes the hesitancy that intent alone may embrace.

The act of caring always alters one's relation to the object of care by awakening and deepening the sense of responsibility for the object of one's care. The action can awaken a sense of responsibility where before there was none or confirms and deepens the interior commitment to care. It can quicken desire and create a sense of urgency.

A. DIRECT ACTION IS ...

- specific, concrete acts of care for the community that engages a person's whole being: mind – body – spirit
- demonstrative care for the well-being of the neighbor
- expressing the natural inclination to care for others that heals both the person who cares and the one who receives the care
- freeing people from their frustrated care, healing the cynic syndrome, making a person whole.
- loving both oneself and others by specific acts of care for others

B. BENEFITS OF DIRECT ACTION

1. Expands Commitment
In my youth the specific, direct act of kissing another person immediately

altered the relationship. Today I guess it takes more to do the same; but the principle is still true. Specific acts alter the interior relationship one has toward the recipient of the action. It may launch one on a journey to deep commitment, just as the first kiss can set one on the way to the altar.

An Asian proverb claims that if you save the life of another, you are responsible for that person the rest of your life. Something like that happens in smaller acts of caring for others. It intensifies our sense of responsibility for the recipient of our care, be it a person, a community, or even a thing. We invest ourselves in the other and the other becomes dearer to us; and we commit ourselves more deeply to its continued well-being. We all want to preserve the value of our expenditure.

The place where we expend our life in caring can deepen in value to the point of becoming sacred space. Expended life hallows the place where the expenditure occurs. It is why we human beings make memorial parks where soldiers have died, as in Gettysburg, where Abraham Lincoln said it well, "We cannot dedicate, we cannot consecrate, we cannot hallow this ground. The brave men, living and dead who struggled here have consecrated it far above our poor power to add or detract."

The same human dynamic is operative in the simple everyday expenditure of one's time and energy. The space where we expend our lives becomes sacred, imbued with the value of our expended lives. Who among us has not longed to return to where we grew up or went to school or where we worked for a significant period of time. And when going there who did not sense the hallowedness of the space, made so by the personal expenditure of one's life and the lives of friends and family.

The expenditure of one's time and energy gives value to that upon which the expenditure is made and so deepens one's commitment. Citizens are often willing to die for their 'Place' and the people in it. It is a final commitment built largely on the sense of the sacredness endowed by the lives that have given it creation and care through the ages.

Any concrete act of care, small or large, will always alter one's relation to the object of care by awakening and deepening the sense of responsibility and personal investment. A concrete act of caring can awaken a sense of responsibility where before there was none. It can also create the appropriate feeling and attitude toward the recipient of the act of care. Action creates resolve that can replace unrealized good intentions. The quicker people get involved in direct action caring, the faster commitment to the community grows and solidifies.

2. Releases 'Those-Who-Care' (TWC)

Direct action is a call to arms. It calls forth Those-Who-Care to pick up the task of being the leaders and workers in the community. Finding Those-Who-Care is not so much a matter of locating these people as it is enabling them to manifest themselves, to become visible, to express their care. Those-Who-Care are always waiting for the opportunity to be engaged, waiting to be called into action and enabled to be effective. Those-Who-Care do not simply appear 'out of the blue.' Nor is one likely to find them by investigating the community by surveys or interviews. They are found when it is time to do something useful. Those-Who-Care decide to involve themselves.

When Those-Who-Care show themselves to each other, they can then organize themselves into a self-consciously, commissioned care force. Direct action releases caring people of any society to become a self-conscious force in the community. Forming this self-conscious body of TWC is the most important goal of the first year of formation. Begin it sooner rather than later. No doubt there are many ways to release care but specific direct action involvement in caring for the community is the best way known to me.

3. Discloses Hidden Realities

Direct action projects uncover new awareness and insights about the reality of the community: its needs, opportunities, problems, quirks, prejudices, openness, blocks, limitations and possibilities. The disclosure of unknown realities will assist the analysis and planning for the future and how to best proceed in the community formation process.

Sartre points out that we never really know the 'truth of our situation' until we begin to act upon it. Many things come to the surface when action is begun that lay dormant until then. A plan is not known to be good until placed in action and corrected by that action, even during the action. Eighty percent of the flight to the moon was spent in course correction.

One community was very welcoming of a development project until some residents were asked go to a leadership training course that was being held in another country. The door of opportunity was slammed shut when the suspicion emerged that the sponsors were trading in slaves or body parts. The trust that appeared to be present in the original reception was in fact not sufficient to overcome this fear.

Another community professed to be open to integration; but when the first black family tried to move into the community, another reality appeared.

I once thought I would be able to skate on ice having been relatively proficient on roller skates; the direct action of stepping out on the ice rapidly corrected my reality picture.

These examples suggest that it is important to begin direct action immediately in order to begin to explore the realities of the actual situation.

4. Heals the Community through Acts of Caring

The physical act of care is a catalyst for healing. The act of giving and receiving of care has a healing affect all around. Sometimes the affection that we know should be there for others is blocked. The action of one's physical body manifesting care for the other in specific acts of caring can release the emotional warmth of affection that may be blocked by the build up of resentment and fear and hurt over the years, thus making us whole. Compassion is released by direct action care.

Cynicism in the community can dissolve in the face of effective direct action involvement. The cynic is always one who cared deeply and was frustrated because there was no way to effectively express his/her care. Cynicism is a defense against the frustration caused by caring and not being able to manifest the care in an effective way. Effective direct action involvement in care dissolves the defense and releases one from the illness of cynicism.

C. MANAGING DIRECT ACTION

1. Genuine Involvement

I am talking of care as a verb, an action, not as an expression of a feeling like saying to someone, "I really care for you." The act is the defining thing, a concrete specific act that cares for the community. Direct action involves the whole person in giving care to the community or individuals. It is more than giving advice, donating money, or participating in community events although those are good also. Direct action involves the investment of one's being in caring for the community. It must cost something in time and energy. It is best expressed as action that involves one's body, mind and spirit. It can be hosting celebrations, decorating the community Christmas tree, volunteering in the preschool, cleaning away garbage, sweeping a street, painting the rocks around the plaza, building a play park, organizing a sports team, cleaning the front of one's house, welcoming new neighbors, or visiting the city authorities to request help for the community.

Involve as many people as possible in the various activities. This gets interchange going on between the workers. Involve as many people as possible in planning as well as execution of the events. Divide the actions into many small jobs rather than have a few people do multiple tasks, both in the preparation for the events as well as the execution.

2. Specific, Achievable and Measurable

These are three important guidelines for direct action. Specific includes having a clearly defined, concrete action. With specific and clear goals participants are able to measure whether that action has been successful or not. If it is measurable, then they are confirmed in their success. Clear definition of the action and careful planning also ensures that the tasks are achievable.

3. Pick Winners

Make sure that you win especially in the early direct action involvement. Choose the battles that have low risk of failure. Plan and prepare the event carefully and in detail to further increase the likelihood of success. In the early formation period go for relatively easy accomplishments that don't require a lot of skill or training. Do things that people know how to do (i.e., cleaning versus building) so that all those who participate leave wanting to do more; and no one leaves with a bad taste in their mouth feeling like they failed.

4. Felt Need

When direct action projects are related to felt need in the community, there is a better chance of success. This motivates residents to involve themselves in the direct action.

5. Celebrate the Action

Always celebrate the completion of an action project, even if it is only stopping to have refreshments at the end of the action. Celebration increases the awareness of the significance of the action and the meaning of their expenditure.

6. Engagement

Engage as many as possible in ongoing programs (e.g., teaching or helping in the school) so they can continue to contribute on a regular basis and for a long period of time. This is the best way to create commitment.

7. Work Projects

Work projects that involve physical labor are one of the best forms of direct action. Few things reveal the character of a person like the stress of physical work. If one is a slough-off or a complainer, it quickly becomes apparent for all to see. If a person is cheerful, helpful and considerate, it too comes out in the work. One sees who is overly concerned with themselves and who is considerate of the whole group, who carries their load, who handles frustration, and who thinks on their feet to discover how to do the work better. One sees who is creatively proactive, and who goes the distance. Physical work projects reveal those who already care and the quality of their being. It may clue in who may become leaders of the community.

Warning

Do not be dismayed if you find yourself promoting doable direct action projects that may seem like a waste of energy because they do not seem to be very valuable accomplishments in and of themselves. Why clean streets when tomorrow they will be dirty again because the community on the whole is a messy bunch? There is value in cleaning the street if it catalyzes deeper commitment and builds the care forces. It can also function as training for leaders, an opportunity to take them on a training journey in planning, organizing and executing a plan. Remember that formation of those who care is the main focus in the first year of community development. Everything is done to facilitate the emergence of the key core of committed workers. Later a structure may be established to keep the street clean with a machine or the city may take over the job and you won't ever have to do it again. But for now it serves a deeper function than just getting things clean (which is also a value even if it is only for a day).

On the other hand, too long a time doing immediately available direct action can get one caught in busy work that wastes energy needed in more important tasks. So it is important to develop, as soon as possible, a long range plan so the direct actions can also serve larger functions by contributing to the realization of long range strategic goals. Cleaning a street in a larger plan could be the launch of a new housing project, for instance, and thus serve double or triple functions. So while direct action is being done, the community must be designing the long range goals and strategies.

Some people believe that every action of care, however temporal in appearance, has a long-range effect beyond our comprehension. It is not my intent to make that case here, only to mention it. It helps to believe that no effort is finally lost. And it does no harm.

CONCLUSION

In summary, to form community someone must elicit from the residents a profound commitment to the community. This is best realized by involvement in direct actions of caring for the community that deepen commitment. When we actively care for someone or something, we become attached to that for which we are caring. When we expend our precious time and energy for something, we develop a self-interest in the well-being of that for which we gave of ourselves. The expenditure of our time, energy, and being flows out of the physical act of caring.

VII. CARE FORCES

Toward Stability

A. Enlisting Those Who Care

B. The Iron Core
1. Solitary self-esteem
2. Service posture
3. Disciplined
4. Self-awareness
5. Open to the new
6. Team player
7. Effectiveness above efficiency
8. Contextually moral

C. The Action Forces

D. The Nurturing Forces

First and foremost community formation happens through the presence of care. It happens when someone decides to care and acts so that care becomes visible, incarnated in flesh and bone. Care is the foundation of formation. Those-who-care (TWC) are the essence of community formation.

Veronica Guerin, an Irish reporter, was horrified by the plight of youth being preyed upon by the drug lords. When she investigated and exposed the deplorable conditions and those responsible in the media, she was threatened repeatedly, beaten, shot and finally murdered. Her incarnated care turned the tide in the drug war and dramatically altered Ireland forever. Her expenditure galvanized the nation into action, sending thousands into the streets to force the drug lords into seclusion. One week after her death the constitution was changed to give the high court the power to seize unsubstantiated wealth. Witnesses testified and went into the first witness protection program in Ireland. The crime rate dropped fifteen percent that year.

When Gandhi heard the report of an approaching clash in Calcutta that could cost many lives if it continued to build, he immediately left for that city. There he announced to the warring parties that he would fast until his death, or until the warring parties made their peace. Neither party could refuse the care he came to give; and peace was restored.

When people see care being given, it inspires them to care and act. Dramatic acts of caring have a large impact. They inspire us. But the caring that keeps us going is more the common, mundane, every day, small acts of care: getting someone to the hospital, preparing a bowl of soup for the sick, helping start the car when the battery is dead, or sweeping the space in front of one's house to help keep the neighborhood clean.

A. ENLISTING THOSE-WHO-CARE

The primary task of community formation is to locate Those-who-care, assist them in organizing themselves, train them, and insure that they find ways to express their care effectively. Long-range success depends on form-ing Those-who-care into a self-conscious team that is recognized by the community as the leaders and facilitators of the community. Do not attempt formation without this dynamic. Those-who-care is the most important ele-ment for the final success of community creation.

In most communities 10% of the people already care to one degree or an-other. Ten percent may never care so do not worry about those who do not respond. The remaining 80% percent can be awakened to their care and be involved in active caring for the community. The first task then is to identify and engage the 10% who already care and form a team of ' Those-who-care'. (There is some evidence that two percent of the population, effectively orga-nized, can effect dramatic change in a society.)

There are many ways to begin. We have already noted how involving people in direct action is a key way to release the passion of Those-who-care into self-awareness and disclose the quality of their commitment.

Parents of young children almost always care about improving conditions for the future of their children. One inner city community began by sur-veying the neighborhood to locate and invite children to be a part of a new preschool. The preschool's inauguration gave 'permission' to invite people to a general community meeting to begin to gather the caring ten percent. The whole community of 5,000 was invited; a few came. In the second meeting some one proposed that the group sponsor a clean-up day and direct action involvement was begun. Soon residents began to discuss all the problems of the community and how the community could work together to resolve them in weekly meetings. Eventually a comprehensive plan was constructed to begin to attack all the problems of the community, focusing on the key problems that create the many problems.

Other beginnings might involve specific projects: establishing a village industry, opening a health clinic, securing safe drinking water, creating a sports field and sports teams, a youth program, or an irrigation system for the crops. Anything that gives an opportunity for Those-who-care to encounter and interact with one another gets the ball rolling.

Those-who-care generally express their care in one of three ways each of which are needed for an effective community care force. Some are more inclined towards solving specific problems. Others are more interested in nurturing care. A few are interested in doing whatever is needed to care for the community. They will form the essential, foundational, enduring core force that support the other forces and enable them to be effective. They are the determined enabling force and may become the leaders of the community.

B. THE IRON CORE

The essential core forces are those who decide to take upon themselves the full responsibility for the care of the whole community in all its aspects, for now and 'until fate do they part'. They care for the whole ball game - the nurture, the action and all the rest. They join the team with the intent to stay until the job is done and are willing to do whatever is necessary to get it done. They are the deeply committed. They intentionally care for the action and nurture forces, enabling them to be effective. They are the servants of the servants.

The initiator of community formation always has as the 'first, last, and always' most important concern the formation of an enduring core of Those-who-care, those who commit themselves to stand through the thick and thin of the struggle. The major focus of the first year of formation is to identify, sensitize, organize, train, and empower the core forces. Find them and enable them to be molded into a team, committed and commissioned by the community to care for the community. They are the ones indispensable to the long-term success of community formation. They are that-without-which all efforts eventually fade.

In one sense forming this core is the only thing one needs to do to insure the creation of community. This task continues till the end of time. Those-who-care must be constantly renewed, replenished, nurtured and matured in commitment. The initiator of community formation is primarily a team builder and coach, the nurturer of the iron core.

For short-term projects involving a few people, a single person can provide the essential core dynamic. For the long march of community formation, it is essential to have a team of committed people to insure continuity, to handle the complexity of today's world, to keep all the plates spinning, to withstand the pressures, to give mutual support, and to avoid burnout. They must care for each other as well as the action and nurturing forces. For every 100 action/nurturing forces, one needs a minimum of five core personnel. Do not continue long without this dynamic or the work will not long endure.

Enlisting the enduring core is not likely to be realized rapidly, but begin it at once. The core could appear 'full blown' in the early days of action; but that has not been my experience. However, be assured, the potential core is already present. Sometimes it takes a long time before individuals mature in commitment. Sometimes it takes weathering a crisis to produce the mature core. Sometimes it is a slow and steady development toward responsibility through careful awakening and education. Sometime it flowers during training in the abilities and skills needed for leading the community. Sometimes it simply means developing, in those who already care deeply, the confidence that they can do the job, or releasing the courage to assume responsibility, to dare to take up the weight of the responsibility. Sometimes the people you think are 'the ones' disappear and other unsuspected ones emerge.

It may be that elected officials will manifest the qualities of long term commitment needed to form the essential core. A town council may be part of the core since they obviously care enough to accept office. Also it is possible that business leaders have to play this role because of their long term self interest in seeing the town thrive and also because of their inherent administrative skills. Be open to all sectors of the community to find and nurture the essential core.

I repeat, the single most important factor for long-range success is growing to full bloom the core team. These people do not have to be great and charismatic leaders, but look for certain enduring qualities:

1. Solitary Self-Esteem

Most important is a sense of self-value that is not in bondage to other influences such as being appreciated and adored by others, possessing wealth or anything else that defines or controls their sense of self-worth apart from their own decision. They answer only to themselves in free responsibility. They are in possession of the power of their own being. They keep their own conscience. Because they are solitarily valuable within themselves, they can be in relationships with a team without destroying the team because they do not have to derive their self worth from being a part of the team. They can stand alone; therefore they are free to be in interdependent relationships without 'selling their soul' to that relationship. Since they do not draw their sense of worth from being a part of the team, or from doing some good deed and feeling good about it, they cannot be blackmailed or diverted from the task at hand.

Since their value does not depend on accomplishments or recognition, they do not have to receive credit or recognition to sustain them. They are free to play any role necessary, large or small that insures the job gets done. They can go anywhere, do any task that is needed and morally permitted to insure the success of the community. Enabling the emergence of this sense of intrinsic self worth in ' Those-who-care' is the first order of the day. This sense of worth may be all that is needed to release the essential core into full bloom.

2. Service Posture

The core forces understand that a life lived on behalf of others is finally the most rewarding life. They put the welfare of others and community on equal par to their personal welfare. They live on behalf of the welfare of the whole of creation.

3. Discipline

They keep their promises. They do what they say they are going to do. They have the power to do what they decide to do because they posses the power of their own being.

4. Self-Awareness

They are self-consciously aware of themselves and their abilities, gifts and limitations. They are reflective, able to evaluate themselves honestly, able to look honestly at themselves and choose to love what they see, e.g., the strengths and weaknesses, the good and bad.

5. Open to the New

They are open to new possibilities. They seek and yearn for the new and better way of living. They are willing to venture out and risk themselves for the sake of a new and better life. They are pioneers on behalf of humankind.

6. Team Player

They are willing to stand together for the long march, through the stress and strains as well as the triumphs, until the job is done. They participate in the give and take of working together. They submit to the accountability of the group. They are able to forgive their colleagues and receive their own forgiveness. They do not have to always be right. Commitment to the mission overcomes conflicts of interest or personality.

7. Effectiveness Above Efficiency.

They endure the frustration of deciding to be effective when it conflicts with being efficient. They are concerned first with what is important to do and secondly with the urgently pressing need. They can prioritize the needs to do what the whole requires not what the individual immediate situation is screaming that one do. They are patient with others.

8. Contextually Moral

They take the long view. They are not tied to immediate or cultural morality. They keep their own conscience and act out of a comprehensive context of 'what is being required by all of history and the whole globe' rather than what others expect or demand.

Forming the enduring core usually is done in and through the forming of the other two forces the nurturing and action forces. In participating in these responsibilities the enduring core force emerges and matures in commitment.

C. THE ACTION FORCES

The action forces start by committing a limited amount of time for specific, concrete tasks to solve a specific problem such as repairing holes in the road, creating a community park, or setting up a preschool. This caring involves individuals self-selecting at different levels of commitment and giving varying amounts of time.

The action forces can eventually be organized into ongoing action teams based on interest, willingness, abilities and skills. Team tasks could be things like: housing renovation, community health care, youth development, community security, arts and crafts, elders care, preschool program, drama club, community literacy, community cleanliness. The action forces can eventually evolve into permanent structures for the community (e.g., an employment agency, community maintenance team, business association, or medical clinic).

In the beginning the action forces need the core forces to initiate the work, call for their help, and guide the work. As the action teams grow, they need the iron core forces to sustain them and call them back to the task. The iron core sees that the work of the action teams fit into an overall plan of the community so their energy is focused into the tasks that are strategically important for the moment and therefore most effective.

D. THE NURTURING FORCES

Some individuals are more inclined toward nurturing rather than problem solving projects (although they may do both). They are people-oriented people. Their vocation is to see that no one is overlooked, that everyone is included. They are like the host or hostess of a party, who makes sure everyone is welcomed, properly served and made to feel like an important part of the party. They are like the nurse, who cares for the patients after the operation has attacked the problem. They are like the matchmaker, who sees that every eligible unwed person finds a partner. They are the big brother or sister, who looks after the younger ones. They are the good neighbor welcoming committee.

They are the first to assist those in need. These people provide a network of care to see that everyone is included who wishes to be included in the care the community provides. If there is a person out of work, these people help get him/her to the community employment agency. They watch over the community to keep the community out of harms way. They create an atmosphere of the community caring for itself. They are the keepers of the community spirit.

Caring people need structures to express their care effectively and be supported in their caring. Without structure, nurturing people are often ineffective and may tend to come off as nosy busybodies. But when organized and focused, they assure that care is given to the total community. The nurturing forces can be organized geographically for more comprehensive and systematic care. There is often a natural grouping of houses that enable the geography to be divided into sectors of about ten houses/families. The community can assign a sector to an individual or team and commission them to know the people in their sector. They become the structure of communication that informs everyone what is going on in the community. In times of crisis they alert the community so each family can take appropriate action. When the community celebrates, they make sure everyone is invited and made to feel welcome. Knowing the needs and concerns of those in their sector, the 'nurturers' genuinely represent their people in the community planning sessions if some cannot attend. If some elect not to participate, they are represented.

From day one, involve Those-who-care in filling the action and nurturing roles for the community. Identify, activate and structure them to be effective in their caring. This attention given to Those-who-care produces high dividends for the time invested. As the community organizer, you must be especially innovative to find ways to care for these care forces – physically, mentally and spiritually. Because of the endless and sometimes poorly defined tasks of care forces, they are especially at risk for burnout. When the time is right, form them into a permanent community organization.

CONCLUSION

It is very easy to get involved in all of the other six whistles and neglect organizing, training and nurturing of Those-who-care. It requires patience and diligence and high intentionality. The temptation is to become involved in solving problems and then put this most important job on the back burner. Those-who-care are the key to the long-term future of the creation of community. It cannot be postponed or left to chance. It must begin the first day of formation. While this is the most important task of the facilitator of community creation, one must, however, blow all seven whistles in order to do this one.

PART TWO

Practical Approaches That Work

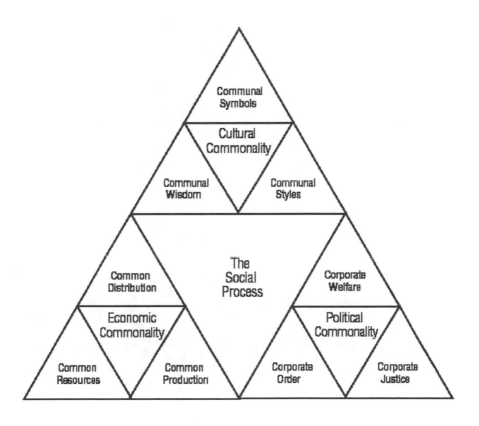

I. COMPREHENSIVENESS

The Foundational Principle

A. Contradiction method

B. Depth human spirit issue

C. Symbol is key

D. Delimited geography

E. Inclusive structures

Among all the principles that guide a viable community formation process, the first and foremost is comprehensiveness. An inclusive, integrated approach is the cardinal assumption of effective formation. A similar awareness is now evident in the realm of Western style healthcare. The increasing emphasis on 'whole person' treatment reflects the growing realization that to provide lasting health it is necessary to deal with the human being as a radically interdependent, integrated system - body, mind and spirit. One part cannot be healthy unless all parts are healthy. A sick stomach sickens the whole person. The interrelatedness of the body is so radical that an acupuncture needle in a mother's foot can cause a baby that is badly positioned in the womb to right itself for correct delivery.

Equally true is the interrelatedness of a community. Profound and lasting health requires that the whole community be involved in attending to all the people and all their problems. Otherwise we end up treating symptoms; healing does not happen. The interrelatedness means that one problem cannot be resolved without affecting other problems and perhaps creating new problems. Some cannot be resolved without first resolving others. Children dying from dysentery could be stopped only when there was safe drinking water. A well for safe drinking water, once realized, required better sanitation facilities to protect the well from pollution. Problems support and feed on each other. Poor housing blocks good health; and poor health keeps one living in shacks. If all the problems are not addressed in dealing with each individual problem, improvements eventually fade.

The inclusion of all the people is essential to healthy community. Each person affects the whole community; and each solitary person is affected by the whole. One man in a formation effort refused to concern himself with the community and its problems. He contended that all his time was needed for his family. When his son became hooked on drugs, he realized that to care properly for his family, he had to care for the community.

The romantic in us is tempted to focus on 'saving the children', to give them a chance. But the fact is that working only with children or youth produces limited success and little long-range results. The adults, who make the decisions that shape the environment in which the children live, can undo in ten minutes the confidence and self-esteem a preschool has spent all day nurturing in the child. However, while little lasting value comes from working only with children, working with children can engage the whole community. A community that focuses on adult development alone loses the inquisitive and inventive spirit of youth and the richness of the elder's wisdom. Without youth, adults diminish their hope in the future and thereby motivation for creating a better community. The community needs the gifts of all ages for full development and profound change. All age groups need the health of the community.

If all the people are not actively or passively involved, formation will not produce the desired benefits and may even be stopped completely as if run into a brick wall. Without full support the community renewal efforts are diminished. It may invite sabotage if some are threatened by the changes. If all the people are not honored in the programming, the community senses that some are 'left out' of the concern of the community, and it sours the stew. The reader knows that if someone dishonors another person in your presence, you begin to wonder if that person dishonors you when you are not present. Likewise, if a community senses that some part of the community is dishonored or neglected, then they begin to wonder if their time will come for being dishonored.

Our lives are bound together by biological, environmental, economic, political, cultural, and spiritual realities to a degree that all are reduced when an individual is diminished; and all are enriched when an individual is enhanced. Healthy community exists when all are well.

Addressing all the problems and involving all the people at the same time is a seemingly impossible task. How can it be done?

A. THE CONTRADICTION METHOD

One way to address all the problems at once is by focusing on the major contradictions of the community. With a clear vision of the desired future of the community and an inclusive analysis of the blocks that are 'contradict-ing' the realization of that vision, the community can discern the four or five underlying, major contradictions that are creating many problems. By attacking these four or five major contradictions, improvement is catalyzed in all the problems areas at once.

In the first community development effort of the ICA, thousands of problems facing the community were identified, and the workers were overwhelmed by the enormity of the task of renewal since we had already decided to deal with all the problems. We were forced to step back and look for what would unlock movement in all the problems. In this way we came to look for the few depth problems that create or support many problems. Then we needed to build a plan to attack those problems. This process was tagged the 'con-tradiction approach'.

When people participate in making the analysis, they see the wisdom of focusing the effort on the few underlying problems. They grasp and appre-ciate that all the issues are being addressed directly or indirectly when the underlying problems are attacked. The result is evident across the board. Inclusive analysis reveals the major contradictions and attacking the major contradictions attacks all the problems at once for all the people.

B. DEPTH HUMAN SPIRIT ISSUE

The most profound way to comprehensively address all the problems and all the people is to address the depth human 'spirit' issue of the community. A broken spirit undercuts all other action and mires the individual and com-munity in hopelessness. When the spirit of the community is negative, little can be done to alter the community. It is the primordial contradiction that formation efforts must always address.

The depth human spirit issue usually manifests itself in a victim attitude – a posture of being victimized by one thing or another. It is always a self-story of insignificance and powerlessness. It is a way of choosing to give away the power of one's being to another force. It is a posture of helplessness, deciding not to be in control of one's life. It is a negation of human freedom and abandonment of responsibility. It is always present when the community is unhealthy.

This victim attitude invades and controls all thinking and action. The victim story becomes the operating story that shapes the perception of reality and therefore shapes all feeling, thinking, deciding, and acting. It is the predisposition for everything one does. If one's operating self-image communicates that one is a powerless victim, then one really *is* a powerless victim.

This image must change if the community is to progress. No one assumes responsibility if they believe they cannot do what is necessary to be responsible. They are predisposed to negate responsibility if they assume they cannot fulfill the responsibility. They may be unable to even dream of a vision much less act to realize one. They have given up their personal power to the victim story.

In an urban community comprised of 95% black residents, the victim image surfaced quickly. Residents told themselves that since they were descendants of slaves, they were second-class citizens without full rights and benefits of the larger society. Guided by this almost unselfconscious story, no one bothered to call the city agency for roads when a huge sink-hole appeared in the road by the storm drain. For years the hole remained, life threatening to small children. When someone finally did decide to act, a single phone call got the hole repaired the next day. The phone call was made because a new story had been told about the value of the people living in the inner city and that they were worthy of the services of the city. It was a new story about the significant contribution of the black race on the nation and globe that altered their sense of value. Black is beautiful was proclaimed in song and community décor. The words in one song echoed their sentiment:

> Deep within the hearts of black men and women,
> Charged by bitterness and pain,
> Burns the spark of human dignity
> That history will claim.

As long as people consider themselves second-class citizens, they will be second class citizens and will content themselves with the poor conditions in their community. When the spirit of the community is negative, little can be done to conclusively alter the conditions of the community. So the formation process must locate the most profound negation in which the community indulges itself and free the community from that negation with a more adequate story and self-image.

The most powerful path to comprehensive formation is to free the human spirit of its bondage to low self-esteem, insignificance, and powerlessness. It makes the difference between the person who says "nothing can be done" and the one that says "all is possible." It is the most important approach to comprehensive, integral development.

C. SYMBOL IS KEY

Symbols are the key to unlocking the shackles of low self-esteem and creating an awareness of value and well-being. Symbols touch our deepest levels of consciousness and enliven our spirit. They unify our being and allow us to participate in reality at the deepest level. Symbols create, focus and internalize our self-stories and thus our understanding of our world, ourselves, and the value and meaning of life

In an inner city community identified by Life magazine as one of the most depressed communities in the Midwest, there lived a large lady with small feet. Whenever she was asked, "How are you?" she enumerated various ailments but invariably the pain in her feet was paramount and a useful dodge for assuming responsibility.

One night in a community meeting the people were discussing how they were going to "keep on keeping on" in the face of the difficult and depressing inner city slum where they struggled to survive against gang warfare, theft, vacant houses, junky streets, deteriorating buildings, drugs, rape and robbery. Somewhere in the midst of the conversation, someone mentioned the passage in the Bible where God says to Jeremiah, "I will make of you an iron pillar" so you can go and do what you have been assigned to do. The group picked up on the image, tossing it around for several minutes before going on to other matters. An artist, sitting in the back of the room, began to sketch an image of an iron person. She later made a miniature iron statue of the sketch and placed it in the center of the next community meeting. The people began to talk about being iron persons. Songs were written and sung, iron man stories told, and iron man pictures were painted on walls. Much later a life-sized iron man statue was erected in the shopping area.

Long before the life size statue was up, the large lady with small feet had begun to volunteer in a newly formed community preschool. One day while visiting the preschool, I asked her how she was. She replied "Fine." "But how are your feet?" says I. "Well," says she, "I have decided not to be tired until I am home in bed."

Only symbols can touch the depths of the human spirit, to heal and to call forth the resolve and the caring that permits the renewal of community. Symbols release interior resources that enable all the people to address all the problems. Symbols hold us before who we have decided to be and create in us that being, enabling us to be who we have chosen to be.

John Kennedy electrified a nation with the symbol of the new frontier and going to the moon. Malachi Martin writes how a smiling Buddha inspired a society to create Angkor Wat. Mahatma Gandhi became the symbol that freed a nation from colonial rule. Symbols are the key to addressing the depth spirit issue and all other issues as well.

D. DELIMITED GEOGRAPHY

Delimiting the operating geography may be necessary to permit a comprehensive approach, especially if one is in a large urban setting. Delimiting the area gives all the people the opportunity to participate in the decisions that affect their lives. Everyone does not have to actively participate; but all need the opportunity and invitation to do so. When people feel they have a way to shape the decisions that shape their destiny, they begin to believe they can 'make a difference' in other ways; and so the task of dealing with all the issues becomes their personal mission. Participation in the planning is especially important. When people shape the vision of the community, they are committed to its realization, actively or passively. When the people 'own the plan', whether or not they actively participate in realizing the plan, the victory is theirs.

Available resources have to be used strategically. One has to decide how and where to place them. It may be necessary to work initially in a smaller area than one would prefer in order to deal with all the problems and all of the people. However, when the resources become available, formation can be expanded.

E. INCLUSIVE STRUCTURES

The creation of inclusive structures, designed to eventually address all the problems, sends a signal that all the issues and all the people are important to the community and the community intends to resolve them all, eventually. They announce that the community is aware and concerned about all the problems and all the people. They are a concrete manifestation of the promise that the community will care for all the people. They are a symbol of the community's resolve and intent to care for all the people and resolve all the problems.

A Guatemalan friend once said to me that he would not vote in the national elections because, "We all know who is going to win." My response was, "That is true and too bad; but still you should vote. Pretending to be a democracy moves a nation toward becoming a real democracy." It creates the expectation in the people of having real representation that becomes a force toward developing democratic structures.

The community puts the structures in place to solve all the problems as 'dream' structures and looks for the time when the dream becomes a reality. They begin to function and grow into the dream. When people imagine and aspire for an eventual solution, they begin to anticipate the solution and that moves them toward a solution. Putting the structures in place fosters the anticipation that solutions eventually will be realized and all people will be served.

The imagined structures place the community on a journey. It puts them 'in training' to deal with all the issues. It is like formulating a dream model in one's mind that creates its own momentum and pulls one toward fruition. It's like playing at a solution until the resources become available and the timing is right for the resolution to occur.

The structures 'created' in the mind at the beginning of formation obviously do not instantaneously appear full-blown, but the community can imagine a full, inclusive image of the structures. One simply creates comprehensive structures out of nothing and announces that they are in being, with specific people assigned to their operation and development. Think of five comprehensive, umbrella structures that cover the many smaller structures needed to bring the community into full formation. At the beginning, four or five small groups can represent and symbolize all the structures that are eventually needed to assure the full functioning of the community. For example, a board of health and education, can hold in symbolic presence the entire myriad of anticipated health and education structures: the preschool, a continuing education forum, a teacher's or parent's organization, a community clinic, health fairs, and doctor visits that serve the community.

Inclusive structures communicate the intention to do comprehensive formation. Establishing them is an act of affirmation that the community can take charge of its life and do what it decides needs doing. It affirms the given situation with a positive, proactive response. When the problems are being intentionally addressed in some way or other, the residents are more patient and hopeful, and willing to contribute to the solutions. It creates the expectation that all the issues are to be addressed. Expectation fosters individual initiative.

CONCLUSION

Profound change occurs only when all the problems are 'dealt with' and all the people are involved in serving and being served. Comprehensiveness is the primary principle of formation. It is the keystone for the overarching philosophy of community development.

TRANSITION TO THREE APPROACHES THAT WORK

It is helpful to divide our thinking about community life into three process-es: the economic, political, and cultural. While remembering that they are in fact one reality, thinking in these three arenas helps one to consider all the aspects of community formation and thus insure comprehensiveness.

The *economic processes* reflect how the community sustains itself in be-ing by using its resources to produce goods and distribute them justly and effectively.

The *political processes* are concerned with how the community organizes itself to maintain order, insure justice and the general well-being of the community.

The *cultural processes* enable the community to grasp the significance and meaning of being a community through shared symbols that embody their self-understanding, through the shared wisdom that embodies their com-mon perception of reality, and through common styles that embody the guidelines that govern relationships and appropriate action.

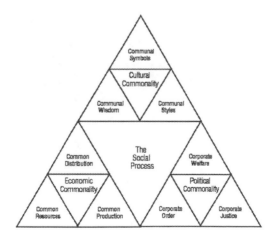

II. POLITICAL PROCESSES

A. The Nod – avoiding unnecessary conflict

B. The Frame – a power base for support and protection

C. Indirection – against powerful foes

D. Total Participation – an inalienable right
   1. Community assemblies
   2. Structural engagement
   3. Community leadership

E. Structures – that rehearse the future

The negative attitude that many have toward politics ignores the natural human necessity to organize ourselves for the common good. Political processes provide order, justice and general well-being for the body politic. Organization and administration necessitates the exercise of power to enforce order and justice. The process involves multiple relationships governed by status and power and subtle maneuvering. The wrongful exploitation of this basic human need gives politics its bad name. It may only be that the abuse of power is more noticeable in the political arena than in the economic and cultural dimension of society.

Five approaches that are helpful for operating in the existing political realities are: the nod, the frame, indirection, total participation, and holistic structuring.

A. THE NOD – AVOIDING UNNECESSARY CONFLICT

People in positions of power can block formation efforts for no good reason except that they were not informed. When formation efforts begin, they may create a real or imagined threat to those in charge, especially when someone unknown begins an activity in their sphere of influence. Any activity they do not know about worries them. Although some blocking may be unavoidable, the 'nod' is a way to avoid unnecessary blocks due to misgivings by the power figures of the community, region and nation.

In community formation the first political action is to locate the power centers and put them at ease by promptly communicating with them before questions, real or imagined, are raised in their minds. Visit them quickly before they become threatened and before the community formation is up and running.

In Guatemala we visited the bishop first, an easy entrée since the church is generally open to listen to whomever. We informed him of who we were, what we intended to do, and invited him to the opening session of the community planning. By informing him and receiving no negative response, we had our nod. We did not ask for his blessing. We shared our information. We asked the bishop whom we should inform about our intended program. He recommended several others, including the state governor. We went to the governor and mentioned that the bishop sent us to see him; it helped insure his nod. From there we continued to the mayor of the municipality. To begin, we asked for nothing, seeking only a 'no objection' nod.

A visit to the army's intelligence center was also necessary since it was dangerous to be identified in any way with a movement that organized people, either left or right. We had heard of people mysteriously disappearing. We gave the receptionist our ICA business card and asked to see the director. We waited for some minutes. When he appeared he seemed tense. After a little time, he relaxed and mopped his forehead when he realized we were from the ICA, the Institute of Cultural Affairs, not the CIA. He was surprised that we asked for nothing and made no objection to our presence.

In the first visit do not ask for anything, not even the nod. You simply give them an opportunity to learn of your presence and intentions in the hopes that they do not express any objection. By not objecting they have given the nod; it is non-verbal, implied by the absence of objection. It is all that is needed to avoid unnecessary blocks.

Never ask for help, approval, support or permission for what you intend to do. Asking for their permission or support is asking them to take responsibility and be held accountable for your actions, a risk they will not take (and should not take) until they know you better. You have no right to ask them to place their political career on the line for you when they do not know and trust you. They can participate in the glory if you succeed; and if you mess up, they are not to blame.

If you even imply that you are asking for approval, they will more than likely give an immediate no, however politely. Besides, you may not want their endorsement until you know you can trust them. However, you can ask for information as that honors and affirms their position of authority.

The visit is not an attempt to test the limits of what they will permit. It is to put the power brokers at ease with your presence. The visit communicates that you intend to work within the structures that exist; you are not out to destroy the existing regime and replace it. The visit honors them and their position. Let them know you intend to keep them informed of your progress and cooperate with them in any way appropriate which again rightfully honors their position of responsibility. Hearing that you intend to keep them informed helps to put them at ease so they can permit things that they might otherwise question. You are helping them to do their job. They will not be threatened unless some change becomes necessary that they may not approve.

If one is working in a community where you have been living for some time, one is likely to assume the right to do whatever one pleases and may neglect this important dynamic. DON'T!!! Get the nod as you begin and avoid a lot of hassle. Getting the nod need not be experienced as a submission of the community to the powers that be.

The visit may later return high dividends beyond just keeping the authorities off your back. In Guatemala the governor of the state adopted the community efforts and blocked the entrance of drug sales. The mayor became a strong supporter especially in getting electricity to the village. In many cases the visit opens the way for them to volunteer assistance later if your success does not threaten their power base. They will give their approval when they see you are doing something good for the community, in which they wish to participate. At that point, when they trust you (and you them), one may be so bold as to ask for assistance.

Again, ask for nothing, not even the nod. Simply inform the authorities in very general terms that are not offensive to them and receive no objection. However, if you get an objection then you have a new situation over which to strategize. You need the frame before returning to visit again.

B. THE FRAME – A POWER BASE FOR SUPPORT AND PROTECTION

The frame consists of people of influence who are willing to lend their influence to the community efforts because they trust and approve of the formation work. They are respected and trusted by the general public and by the 'powers that be'. Their relationship bestows upon the community workers their influence and protection. The old adage is true, it is not *what* you know, but *who* you know. The old boy/ old girl network is a universal social dynamic and everyone needs one. The frame is a power base of authorization, a support network, and the armor that protects one from the wolves.

Although the frame may assist in many ways, its major contribution is lending influence and guidance. With a 'frame' one can move with confidence in the power structures of the community, region and nation. The frame eases the way into the necessary centers of power, opening doors of opportunity, and facilitates the acceptance of the program.

The frame is essential to weather attacks which may come from: a right wing patriot who considers any change a Communist plot, a paranoid government bureaucracy, or people who oppose anybody who is not as timid as they. Someone somewhere is going to be threatened by change which always accompanies formation. (Only babies like being changed.)

The frame is most often composed of individuals, but a 'friend' can also be an organization or institution of influence. If one has recognition from an organization like the United Nations, church, business, or government agency, it can be an important part of one's frame.

In Guatemala, we were helped by the federal government's Reconstruction Committee, which screened non-governmental organizations and then facilitated their work with visas, materials and assisting with special problems. When they officially approved of us, it opened many other doors in the society. One company joined forces with the community to introduce state-of-the-art irrigation systems that they wanted to market in the country and the village wanted for their farmers. A city employee working with marginal communities lent the weight of her office in the municipal government when new programs frightened people.

The frame should eventually include influential friends from all arenas of society – public, private and civic. In the public sector look for individuals who do not disappear after each election or coup d'etat. They will be around for the duration; and they know how to work the system. Look for those able to cut thru bureaucratic red tape when necessary to get something done; but avoid those who depend on red tape to protect their jobs. If you are in a polarized political situation, look for a few friends who are above the fray, who are non-aligned and respected by all factions. People in the medical profession are often above the fray, as we found in Guatemala where a prominent doctor who ran a children's hospital was also part of the aristocracy.

In Chicago the Mayor's Chief Assistant became our friend and then our salvation when riots swept the near Westside of Chicago following the assassination of Martin Luther King Jr. Many non-residential buildings were being burned by a mob. A phone call to him made the police available to us when they were needed in a thousand places at once and probably saved our training center. A local community gang, with whom we had been working, protected us when we had to move around the community in this time of chaos.

Friends in the business world are effective advocates in a society that accords a lot of prestige to the economic sector of society. Look for friends in the local and multinational businesses and all forms of private enterprise. Sometimes the secretary of the CEO can be as much help as the CEO. Business associations with a social conscience like the Rotary Club can often provide a way into the business world. The religious community cannot be overlooked. Don't take sides in this arena but honor all expressions of faith existing in the community. The personnel of some NGOs such as CARE develop a good deal of influence and may often cooperate in projects as well as lend their influence. Entertainers are a powerful force in society and can give a special kind of authorization. University faculties enjoy a special respect from society and thus are valuable friends.

Constant and systematic strengthening of the authorizing frame is essential. To maintain awareness of the need to continue to nurture the frame on its journey, it is helpful to chart the journey of commitment into various levels and list the contacts in a matrix. For example, a person who becomes part of the frame may begin as an interested but hesitant party, and still permit the use of his/her name. S/he may progress to becoming a committed friend of the community, then an advocate, then a patron and finally an active guardian. If you are not aware of where a person is on the journey, you can easily lose their support by asking too much or too little. If you ask someone to assume the role of advocate before they are ready, you may frighten them off. On the other hand, a deeply committed guardian may be hurt if you don't ask enough of them.

Develop the frame matrix as soon as possible. The matrix reveals where the frame is strong and where it is weak. The matrix keeps one self-consciously aware and intentional in developing the frame. It enables one to see opportunities to nurture the frame that might otherwise be overlooked (see Addendum One).

In addition to keeping them up to date with regular reports, it is important to account to the frame for the use of their influence and the effectiveness of the program. Consult with them, seek their advice and welcome all offerings of assistance whether or not they can be used.

C. INDIRECTION - AGAINST POWERFUL FOES

Never attack 'head on' a negative power base that you are not absolutely, positively sure you can beat. Dead may be where you end up if you don't win. Direct confrontation can destroy a community project. Pick the direct confrontation battles you are sure you can win and 'attack' indirectly the negative forces against whom you cannot win in a 'head on' confrontation.

In one urban community there was a small hotel that was a center for prostitution and the distribution of drugs, run by the mafia. Some of the ladies came asking for help from the community. It was painful to say the community was powerless to be of direct help. Had the community mounted a campaign to investigate and arrest the drug dealers, they would have been easily, quickly and decisively crushed. The community would never be equipped to do that job which is the purview of the police.

Instead the problem was attacked indirectly. A medical clinic was opened next door to the hotel that served all community members, including the hotel staff. A community shopping center was built across the street along with a mini-park. Improved streetlights brightened the area. Community sponsored housing reconstruction projects slowly surrounded the hotel. After some time the drug dealers chose to move their operation to where the climate was more amenable to their purposes.

In a non-confrontational manner make it less profitable or less comfortable for negative forces to practice in the community, meanwhile helping where possible those victimized by the negative forces. Pick the overt battles you can win; win the others with indirection; and learn to tell the difference.

D. TOTAL PARTICIPATION – AN INALIENABLE RIGHT

Every person has the right to participate in decisions that affect his/her life. Participation creates a sense of being in charge of one's destiny that is essential for the experience of self-worth and one's capacity to assume responsibility for the future. It creates a sense of hope for a better future and motivation to realize that future.

Of course everyone cannot participation in every community decision; it would paralyze operations. Some must be given the power to decide on behalf of the community. However, everyone deserves the opportunity to participate in forming the context in which the decisions are made, that is to say, all must agree on the vision, the basic values, the guiding principles of operation, the community constitution if you please. And regular account-ability must be held to insure adherence to the operating context set out by the whole. At the very least everyone should have the option of being heard by those who make the decisions.

Not everyone will participate; but everyone must have the opportunity to do so. The choice must be theirs. If they do not take the opportunity, they are participating by deciding to let others make the decisions for them. The following are three ways to engage community participation.

1. Community Assemblies

A community-wide assembly dynamic is needed two to four times a year where everyone is invited. The four essential parts of the assembly are (1) the leaders accounting to the community for past decisions and actions; (2) the participative visioning by all of the desired future; (3) the honoring of every individual attending in one of various ways; and (4) celebration.

We began village community formation projects with a week of planning in which every family in the village participated. For those who did not come to the planning session, interviewers were sent daily to visit every home to ask about the future the villagers wanted and how the community could go about realizing those dreams. The return in motivation and commitment to the formation of the community was well worth the effort.

When people participate in the planning, they own the plan and it becomes their responsibility to see that the plan is actualized.

2. Structural Engagement

Offer the opportunity, for everyone who chooses, to participate in working to actualize the vision of the community assembly. This requires organiza-tional structures to enable effective action, namely nurturing and problem solving structures described in Chapter VII. Both forces need specific, con-crete structures that enable them be effective. Look for structures that are different from the president, vice president, secretary, and treasurer that harks back to the top down, bureaucratic images of the past. Think of a 'bottom up' organization structure where consensus of the whole is as influential as the influence of the powerful.

3. Community Leadership

As soon as possible the community needs a self-consciously agreed upon focus of leadership that integrates the community and facilitates the formation of a community identity and loyalty. It needs a way to coalesce, grow together, unite, integrate, converge, and congeal a focus of power to act effectively. It needs a genuinely representative body and a symbolic leader that is acknowledged and accepted as being an expression of the will of the community.

The management dynamic can be a person or a group. However, if a group is seen as the managing dynamic, a first among equals often emerges to help symbolize and focus the community identity. These people provide 'glue' that holds the community together and also maintain a comprehensive perspective for the community. They facilitate and coordinate interaction, and give substance and structure to inter-relationships. They are the ones out in front in the sense of inventing the next steps in the development of the community.

Among the first structures for the development team to set in motion, is a body of individuals who can represent the whole community and perhaps will become the leadership dynamic of the community. If there is already a formally elected body of leaders, then they must become the formation council or appoint a committee to work with the formation team. If no leadership is formally established, look for the acknowledged elders of the community who have informal power to speak for the members of the community. Or create an informal election process such as representatives from various parts of the community geography, or formally elect a community council to represent the community.

The council may not immediately receive the respect of the community; but as the council goes about caring for the community in small ways, it will emerge with the respect and backing of the community. They grow into the reality of being a real manager of the affairs of the community; and the community grows into accepting the council leadership. The structure reflects possibility by its mimicry of the real thing. The reflection calls the reality into existence.

This unifying dynamic must flow from the bottom-up, not an appointed top-down by authority figures. It must be open for new persons to flow in and some to drop out as the community expresses its will, without falling into a struggle of conflicting egos. No status for status sake, power must accompany responsibility and responsibility must accompany power. They go together if it is to work. As much as possible distinguish between the administration functions from the symbolic leadership function, which maintains the comprehensive perspective and leavens the administration.

In addition to needing a focus of power to act effectively, the community also needs a balance of power to assure justice and general well-being. There has to be a 'court of appeals' to correct the errors of those in power and temper the exercise of influence. Everyone needs to know where to go if they have an issue that is not honored by the leadership.

Many unjust treatments are oversights and not intentional abuse by the leadership. There must be safeguards against both the intentional and the unintentional abuse of power by some by the structures of the community. Sometimes individuals who have the power to intervene and correct the problem handle this informally. It is better to have a structure to do this job like a complaint department does it for a store. In communities it could be a designated committee or a person of influence in each sector of the community to hear the cry of those left out of the care of the community.

E. STRUCTURES - THAT REHEARSE THE FUTURE

To sculpt a community organization, begin with the whole in mind and envision an organization that will reflect the desired future of the community. Conceive of an ideal set of structures and announce that it is symbolically in being. Create a dream organization and with time grow into a realization of the dream, guided by the imagined structure.

When one builds a house, s/he first must have a plan or at least an image of what is going to be constructed. Without the plan it is hard to know where or how to begin the construction. Concrete, specific images of possibility call us to action. Without the envisioned structures, there is no impetus to move rapidly to a viable development of the community possibilities.

Begin with the best possible design of the desired structures that the community can conceive. Then set up the envisioned structures rudimentarily. The community then grows into a manifestation of the envisioned ideal structure. The development process of course alters the conceptions, but without the vision of the appropriate structure nothing is likely to happen. Vision precedes actualization.

The reader no doubt has seen individuals who grow into their job. They grow into the structure into which they have been placed and to which they have committed themselves. Presidents are sometimes a dramatic demonstration of this dynamic. They may not be as 'presidential' as they could have been when elected; but they seem to grow more rapidly when 'structured' into the driver's seat of the office. Their learning curve goes up as they see things in a new perspective and are more highly motivated. They grow to match the needs of the structure into which they have been placed, becoming more presidential (most of the time).

Have you not experienced committing yourself to something and discovered that you personally grew more rapidly following the commitment? Assuming responsibility for something intensifies one's living, one's intellectual focus, and one's emotional control. Commitment releases interior resources and focuses one's being. It amplifies the available interior resources needed to do the job. A conceived structure, however rudimentary, enables commitment to be made by those who care.

The community can conceive and 'establish' the envisioned structures to which they 'marry themselves', and grow into the reality that the envisioned structure' symbolizes. (Something like this must be what happens in arranged marriages.) The 'imagined structure' mimics a reality that may not yet exist but that is desired, so it calls the community to actualize the dream that the envisioned structure symbolizes. The community grows into the envisioned structure. A commitment to the invented structures calls the community to actualize the structure that has been imagined and articulated. Feeling at first like actors, they 'play' at being an organized community until they grow into being an authentically organized community. The flawed practice of a desired ideal enables the desired reality to emerge.

Create structures like the better business committee, celebration committee, lyceum of arts, legal aid association, employment agency, community health clinic, effective living information center, civic mobilization committee for effective suffrage, community promotion agency, college of lifelong education, local security guard force, or human rights information center. Begin with whatever structures the community conceives is needed to be a fulfilling community for everyone and begin putting flesh on the vision. Do not wait for perfected, full-blown, 'real' structures before beginning operations. Begin with the whole in mind, and with whatever is there is on the ground to use. How many stories have we heard about a massive business that began in a garage?

CONCLUSION

Structural Revolutionaries: The political process is the way the community organizes itself and assigns authority and power to bring order, justice and general well-being to all the community. The formation team takes into account the power relationships that exist in the community, municipality, state and national structures, and finds ways to operate creatively within them, hopefully enabling them to evolve to more effectively serve the community.

The alternative is to step out of the existing structures, call for a revolution that removes the old structures and then build new ones, a very difficult task indeed, especially building the new ones. In the long run, destroying the existing systems is rarely helpful except in cases where the powers have become a closed and evil system such as Hitler's Germany. The better approach has always been to seek ways to operate within the existing structures with an eye to recreating the structures from within, to be a leavening force that enables the structures to evolve more humane and creative forms that provide a better way of life for all creation.

I was intrigued by the story a Brazilian told me about the revolution that separated Brazil from Portugal. My Brazilian friend said the king and family had been in Brazil to escape the conquering army of Napoleon. As the king prepared to return to Portugal and reclaim his throne, he advised his son who was to remain in Brazil, "If the people get restless and want independence from Portugal, you declare the 'revolution' and yourself as president." And so the independent nation of Brazil was born and did not have the violent struggle that scarred many South American nations.

I think that it is something like the enlightened 'revolution' that formation is seeking – one that reads the signs of the times and gets in step with the next level of the creative evolution of human civilization.

III. ECONOMIC PROCESSES

A. Building Wealth – turn the money over nine times

B. Infusion of Money – from anywhere

C. Protect the Local Economy – from money drain and outside exploitation

1. Guard existing resources
2. Counter market invasion
3. Husband the reserves

D. Integration – into the larger economy

Life is sustained through the economic processes whereby the available resources are used to produce goods that are distributed to the people. The economic process is foundational in that all other concerns are irrelevant unless a community is sustained in being. Minimally, the community must feed, house, and provide health care for its people.

A. BUILDING WEALTH
TURN THE MONEY OVER NINE TIMES

A major issue in the economic development of most developing communities is that the money entering the community does not stay in the community long enough to create wealth. Wealth is created when money circulates to benefit as many people as possible before it exits the community. Wealth is diminished when the profits and cash go too fast out of the community to buy outsider's goods rather than remain in the community to buy goods and services produced by the community members.

When I lived in Peru, I deposited my money in a neighborhood bank. The bank used my money to make more money for itself and paid me a pittance interest on the capital. The owner of the bank took the earnings and spent them in another community where he lived. Thus the value of my capital left my community to create wealth elsewhere. In earlier times a bank owner lived in the community where the bank operated. He bought his food, attended programs, entertained guests in his home, thus spending his money in the community where the bank was located. Now the owner rarely lives in the community where the bank is located; therefore the lion's share of the capital profits leave the community to be spent in another community, or maybe even another country. The price of living in a global economy is that much of the money leaves the local community before it can create wealth for the residents.

Wealth is created when someone working outside the community brings his money into the community to buy something at the local grocery; then the grocer goes to the local barbershop and spends that dollar for a haircut;

then the barber takes the dollar to the local bakery and buys some bread; the baker hires the local mason to build an additional oven for his store; the mason buys some beans grown by the local farmer, who goes to the café to buy his lunch with John's dollar; and the restaurant owner buys a rug made by a local resident, who then buys a dress made by the village seamstress, who places it in a local cooperative credit union -- and so on. Many different people benefit from the same dollar brought in from outside. When the money goes around and around in the community before it goes out, then the community begins to create wealth.

One of the first tasks in revitalizing the community's economy is to look for ways to keep the money circulating as long as possible before it leaves the community. Try to turn it over nine or more times. Look for where the money is leaving and see if there is a way to provide the product or services that the people are getting from outside. Look first at the basic needs (e.g., bread) and essential services (e.g., health care). Then look at other services (e.g., haircuts), to see if they can be provided within the community. Be creative and think long-range in economic planning. It may take some time to alter the situation.

In one village the bread for the community was produced in the neighboring town five kilometers away. So the purchase price not only included the cost of production but also transportation to the village. The community found and assisted a person who wanted to establish a bakery. With a small capitalization the daily expenditure for bread, both production and consumption, stayed in the community to create wealth.

Some communities have experimented with creating 'community money' to prevent the exit of value. In this system certain jobs are assigned a value. Then chits, issued by the community, can purchase those services. Sally gets five chits for baby-sitting an hour and she can go to the drugstore and buy some ice-cream and the ice-cream man can use the chits to get a haircut. Setting up their own 'currency' guarantees the circulation of the 'money' [value] within the community. This practice takes managerial effort to facilitate the process. The barter system is a similar process that keeps value in the community. A more widely practiced process is the credit union. It can guard the profits made from the capital of its members and return it to the community members.

In another community its members bought a farmer's produce before it was planted. The consumers thus participated in the risks the farmer normally takes to produce the food and the farmer gave the consumer a better price and better product. It helps to guarantee the continuation of the small farmer tradition and keep the value in the community. It avoids paying for the transportation, which is a large part of the cost of the produce bought in a supermarket. It cuts the cost of the middleman. It also gives the consumer a healthier product since it was grown without insecticides or chemical fertilizers.

In more complex communities where the services are done on a 'Wal-Mart principle' (the bigger the store the cheaper the prices), keeping the money in the community is more difficult. This necessitates even more creative approaches. Specialty stores sometimes can compete with the big retailers by giving personalized service. One can also try to convince Wal-Mart owners to recognize their responsibility to contribute to the well-being of the communities from which they take their profits by sharing in the cost of maintaining the community infrastructures.

B. INFUSION OF MONEY – FROM ANYWHERE

Obviously, a community needs to bring in money to circulate. Working in jobs outside the community is the tried and true way to bring money into a community. A community can establish a job search structure like an employment agency to facilitate this process. One community established a school that prepared people for better jobs. The first task in the school was to improve the self-images of the participants. On the other side of a repaired self-esteem the students more easily absorbed the training in the basic skills needed in the work place. The final training process developed skills to interview for a job. New self-esteem also developed the courage to find, and the determination to keep, a job. The program also included nurturing a network of employers who came to trust the people who came out of the program.

Sometimes the community possesses a resource that is desired by the outside world if it is properly marketed. One agricultural and fishing village found that one of the things that the farmers considered a major problem turned out to be marketable. They had an excess of rocks that made it necessary to plant the fields by hand. However, when cut, the rocks made beautiful building stones. All that was required was a diamond saw and an income producing business was born to supplement the fishing and farming income. At the same time, it improved the condition of the farmers' fields.

In another village it was the resource of a wonderful climate and lots of sunshine and the happenstance of being near an overpopulated city. The village provided a wonderful place to get away for a few days. Weekend 'vacations' boosted the village economy.

Another community seemed to have no recognizable resource beyond the people, so people became the resource that was marketed by contracting 'piece work' with a company. The company provided the needed materials and transport. The villagers provided the labor to produce a product and were paid for their labor. The company needed the product; and the village needed the income.

In another village a furniture industry was easily begun to make furniture out of wicker. In the nearby city a business woman wanted the furniture produced so she capitalized the beginning of the industry, trained the workers, and handled the marketing. The frame can be helpful in finding these opportunities.

In another village the farmers focused on increasing their production with state-of-the-art drip irrigation that enabled them to more than double the number of crops per year and produce five to seven times higher yields per crop. They managed to get a guaranteed market for tomatoes from a nearby salsa factory increasing the farmers' income ten-fold.

Grants are another way to bring in money; but they should be used to improve the economic production process, to produce more with the available resources in order to move toward economic self-sufficiency. Of course, grants may also be used to improve the economy indirectly, for instance, by improving the health of the community (e.g., safe drinking water) so residents are stronger and more able to improve their economic situation.

C. PROTECT THE LOCAL ECONOMY – FROM MONEY DRAIN AND OUTSIDE EXPLOITATION

1. Guard Existing Resources
Community resources can be acquired and exploited by outside forces who take the profits and leave. An early job is to analyze thoroughly the community resources to see what is available to produce income, and guard them carefully. Protect the community's land, mineral rights, human resources, its rights and privileges that provide economic advantages, its reputation, and its production capabilities.

Outside forces can undercut the community by luring away needed human resources. Capable people are sought for other jobs. People's time and energy can be sucked away by wasteful pursuits that do not leave time for building a viable community economy. The local talent can be nurtured and honored to stay loyal in the face of more lucrative or diversionary offers. Do this by clarifying the importance of the mission of the community, its history-long, worldwide value. Work that is significant withstands the lure of lucrative offers.

2. Counter Market Invasion
A village or community market is vulnerable to being targeted by outside forces. The money can be drained by scams that entice spending for items

that are inappropriate to the economic needs of a developing economy and drain off the wealth of the community.

The community market can be exploited in ways that local people cannot compete. One community established its own bakery, which was undercut by a bakery in a nearby larger community. The outside bakery reduced prices below cost of production for a time and offered a larger variety to discourage the local bakery. So the bakery had to refine its product and look for long-term capitalization to compete and offer better services. Providing better services and better products is the way to counter outside forces, not by blocking needed services from outside.

A more difficult approach is to tax outside vendors for the use of the community infrastructure. Those who take money out of the community are asked to share the cost of maintaining the community infrastructure that gives them a place to market their wares (e.g., streets, lights, garbage, parks, or storage).

3. Husband the Wealth Reserves

Take care that the money and resources that exist in the community are spent well, especially when spent outside the community. Insure that the community gets fair value for its expenditures and maintains sufficient reserves for emergencies and for needed research, expansion and development. Cooperative buying in bulk is one way to get more for each dollar. Often sensitive businessmen give community development projects a sizable reduction in prices.

D. INTEGRATION – INTO THE LARGER ECONOMY

When all has been done to protect the local economy, then look to be a responsible part of the larger economy, contributing to it and enjoying its benefits. Local economies have a responsibility to the larger economy; and the global economy has a responsibility to and for the local community. The two economies need each other. The local economy needs the larger economy to provide values that are not possible to create on a local level. A university education, or a superb hospital or an airline service cannot be supported by the economy of one local community. One can list hundreds of benefits of being part of the larger economy. The community needs the larger market to support local industry that the local market alone cannot sustain.

Local economies need the global economy to avoid becoming ingrown and sterile. The community economy needs the cross-fertilization beyond its borders to develop a creative entrepreneurial mindset. The larger economy is necessary to the prosperity of the community and to prevent becoming ingrown and retarded.

On the other hand, without the local economies the larger economy would exist only as an abstraction. The city, state, and national economy depend on the local for its well-being. If the economy of the local communities breaks down, it becomes impossible to sustain the general economy. Just as the health of the body depends on the health of its parts, so the society as a whole depends on the health of individual communities. Thus, it behooves the larger society to be concerned about the economic health of the local communities.

Local economies should take their place in the larger fabric when they are able to do so, when they have the basic economic structure to survive and can both contribute and profit from participating in the larger economic structures of society. They have the responsibility to do so; and it can be done on a basis of mutual respect and support.

CONCLUSION

To develop economic well-being in a community, money coming in and circulating at least nine times will create wealth. The community must protect its resources, its means of production, and distribute the wealth in an equitable manner. At the same time, the community must seek to participate in the larger economy in a mutually supportive relationship.

IV. CULTURAL PROCESSES

A. Liberating Environment
   – exterior and interior dynamics

B. Symbols – profound communication

C. Story – the key symbol

D. Refreshing Celebrations

E. Shared Mission

F. Unending Education – formal and informal

A community flourishes if it has a healthy culture that imbues it with significance, communicating to everyone why it is worthwhile to work to sustain community and organize to protect it. The culture binds the individuals to the community for deeper reasons than physical sustenance and mutual protection.

The culture of a community is embodied in the community's common wisdom, style and symbols. The common symbols reveal the deepest meanings of being an individual in a community. The common style defines what is appropriate, morally and socially. It tells us how to act, how to dress, and how to relate to one another, guiding everyday life in the community. The common wisdom spells out what is a fulfilled life. It defines our perception of reality which provides the foundational context and perspective for living a life together. To nurture the cultural life of communities there are six approaches which work

A. LIBERATING ENVIRONMENT – EXTERIOR AND INTERIOR DYNAMICS

The shared environment always requires careful attention because of its pervasive power to form the community consciousness and thus the culture of a community. The environment unceasingly bombards everyone with images of significance or insignificance, informing the residents of their value or disvalue.. People are constantly brainwashed toward freedom or bondage by the images that are created by the physical space around them.

When you last walked into a five star hotel, you may recall how the space created within you a sense of well-being, of being valuable. When you walk into a slum with broken windows and a dirty, trashy street, you have the immediate feeling of being unwelcome, of being out of place, of diminished personal value.

When the ICA moved its headquarters to the near west side of Chicago, we had to constantly resist the tendency to become depressed because the environment communicated that deterioration was winning, that things were out of control. One had to be highly intentional with personal space to counter the messages of the outside environment.

A community's consciousness is formed by whatever messages are daily bombarding their awareness through the living environment. The people eventually come to believe what the space is communicating about them. It happens on a conscious or unconscious level. If the community space is ugly, disorganized, or junky, individuals come to think of themselves as ugly, disorganized, incomplete, and of little value. If the space is orderly, clean, and pleasing, then the community's spirit is confident of being in control of life and living.

On a Caribbean island where I went to give a seminar, the moment I entered the town I knew there was little sense of community. The houses were beautiful and well kept; but the streets and public spaces were a mess. It was individual families living in proximity with little sense of community. The space revealed the existing isolation and helped maintain the separation.

In contrast, I remember vividly a visit to Mother Teresa's Sisters of Charity Center in a Lima, Peru slum. The Sisters cared for the hopelessly poor and terminally ill of the city. The setting was bone poor and nakedly bare, but the cleanliness and the highly intentional form given to space by simple acts, like placing whitewashed stones in the courtyard to define a passage way, communicated to whoever entered the center a sense of being cared for, of being valued.

When we give seminars, we keep the space simple and modest, but give very careful attention to details like how the tables are arranged, the way the chair colors are set together, the way the table servings are set with each knife, fork and spoon in perfect alignment, the way the walls are decorated. When the participants enter the room they are immediately aware that they are valued because someone cared enough to arrange their space with high intentionally.

The reader no doubt has read or heard how spirits are broken by solitary confinement or other space deprivation techniques that deprives one of affirming space. Negative space creates negative beings; positive space builds confidence.

One of the first concerns in cultural formation is to see that the common space communicates that everyone is important as individuals and as a community. Many different things can improve the message that the space is sending.

In the first week of a village formation project, sizable stones were used to define a future plaza and painted with whitewash. Before there was an open space where the horses and an occasional car passed indiscriminately. With the rocks defining a future plaza, the traffic had to follow the streets; and the people had a place to pause and visit with one another. The simple act of defining the future plaza immediately lifted the spirit of the community.

In an inner city community the residents organized one block and assisted every family in painting the fronts of their houses in one week. It made a powerful demonstration of how space can uplift the community spirit.

In another urban community mini-parks were created, often with only enough space for one bench and a flowerbed.

A simple playground for the children, created with discarded light poles, became an 'art-like' park for another community and gave the children a place to play.

Anything that gets the space screaming that the community and its residents are valuable lifts the spirit of the community. Ask yourself what is the common space saying about the community, about who they are, their value, their significance, their mission, and how best to live a full-filled life.

B. SYMBOLS – PROFOUND COMMUNICATION

Of equal priority in forming cultural 'strength' is the renewal of existing symbols or the birthing of new and more adequate symbols of value and significance. People with strong symbols can withstand space deprivation and override spatial brainwashing. Symbols, more than anything else, address the deeps of our consciousness and inform us of our value. They address our entire being, far below our conscious awareness, on the physical, mental and spiritual levels. They enable us to 'participate in the reality to which they point.'

When we decide who we want to be and then create symbols to remind us, we are enabled to steadfastly be whom we decided to be and do what we decided to do. They hold in place our being. They renew our awareness about whom we choose to be and what we choose to do.

While working with an Aboriginal community in Australia, the formation team was obviously doing the correct actions necessary for development but the development lacked vitality. Then one morning the elder told of his dream, the symbol for which the people were waiting and the project took off. The effect was electrifying, the place came alive; and the programs began to dance with infused life and life flowed into and out of the work and play.

C. STORY – THE KEY SYMBOL

Probably the most important symbol is the inclusive story of the significance of the community that was presented in the chapter on Storytelling. I mention it again here to reemphasize its importance for the cultural life of the community.

The story is important because we are, and constantly become, the story we tell ourselves. We are constantly recreated, renewed, and held in being by and through the stories we tell ourselves about who we are and what we are doing with our life, and why we do what we do. Renewal can come from recovering an old story or creating a new story that captures the imagination of the community. "We learn our ways of being and reinforce our values by telling tales about each other."

We all know people who live out of an "I can't" story that permeates every moment of their lives. It has many forms: "If only I were smarter ... I'm not equipped to ... my wife does not want me to ... I really can't be bothered ... I don't have the resources ... people don't like me ... I'm too old ... I'm too young ... I was born in the wrong time." Others have a self-story that tells them, "I can do anything to which I set my mind." All are self-fulfilling prophecies, for individuals and for communities; they energize or demoralize. Someone with an 'I can' story is far more energetic and creative than someone living out of an 'I can't' story.

I have a friend that always answers the greeting, "Hello, how are you?" with the answer, "Great, couldn't be better." I have another friend who answers the same greeting with a rundown of the latest problem he's having. The first is always full of energy; the second is always slightly off full energy. These daily rituals rehearse our self story and shape how we relate to life in general and the particular moment.

In a U.S. inner city preschool the teachers taught the children to sing:
> "I am always falling down;
> But I know what I can do.
> I can pick myself up and say to myself,
> 'I'm the greatest too.'"

Learning to tell that story to themselves avoided a lot of crying. It helped that they could borrow "I'm the greatest!" from Cassius Clay, who was then the current world champion boxer who happened to be the same color. His story, no doubt, augmented his fighting abilities.

In any given moment, the problem is not the external situation; but the way we relate to it. The story we tell ourselves shapes the way we relate to both the positive and negative experiences of our lives. It both reflects and creates an attitude toward life at the same time. The story can drain the life out of the community or it can empower the community to greatness.

I heard of a thirty-year old woman who for years told herself, "I am an illegitimate child," a story told her by her parents. Her society labeled such a child a 'bastard', a word often used to curse or ridicule. Brainwashed by her society to think of herself as despicable, it was not surprising that she lived a negative and depressing life. One day before she decided to jump in front of a subway car, it occurred to her that she was no longer a child, and that being illegitimate was of her parents doing and should have no power over her. That left her with only the story, "I AM", breaking the spell of depression and releasing her to new life.

If one wishes to conquer and subjugate a people, one only has to take away their stories by removing the storytellers. The community eventually forgets who they are, what they want or deserve and why they are valuable. Instead they embody the story of the conqueror and become the conquerors' obedient subjects. They lose their identity and adopt the one given them.

In the book *Ishmael*, author Daniel Quinn takes issue with one of the ancient stories of the Judeo-Christian faith. He points out that the part of the creation story that commands man "to have dominion over all the creatures that walk and fly" is now a limiting story if taken literally. He would prefer a more inclusive story to guide humankind and prevent men from destroying the environment and all the creatures that walk and fly, including humankind – a story that proclaims the rights of all the creatures of the universe. Perhaps a more appropriate story would be one that says the earth belongs to all life on the planet and humankind is commissioned to love and care for it all.

D. REFRESHING CELEBRATIONS

When asked, "What is the meaning of life?" the revered guru answered, "*that thou art.*" The wisdom of the guru is ritualized in celebrations that drama-

[1] *Ishmael: An Adventure of the Mind and Spirit*, Daniel Quinn, 1992, Bantam/Turner Books

tize that we most definitely and assuredly *are* valuable in every moment. Celebrations affirm that it is good to be, to have life. They imbue life with meaning 'in and of itself' proclaiming that life as it is given is immensely valuable. What can be more important than having life? Celebrations rehearse the joy of being alive, recreating and imparting life. The fact of life is the meaning of life.

Because celebrations affirm life, they are a pathway to the interior freedom to assume responsibility for the life we have. By reminding us that life is good, celebrations call us to live it fully, 'just as it is', as pure meaning. Celebrations pronounce absolution on the past and affirm the future as open and full of possibility. They bring closure to difficult periods of life. They open ways to begin anew. They enable people to reveal themselves and be accepted as they are, healing broken relationships.

Good community celebrations rarely just happen. Rather they take significant expenditure of time and energy to create them. Careful preparation and committed facilitation is needed to see that every person is involved and cared for in the event. A good celebration begins when the first person arrives, and closes while everyone is having a good time so everyone will want to come back again. So end the event intentionally while all are still 'enjoying' the event. They will return with a positive anticipation for the next one. A few serious moments of reflection or heightened awareness somewhere toward the end of the event deepens the experience of celebration. Involve as many community members as possible in preparing and hosting the celebration. Be sure all feel welcomed. The space décor is fifty percent of creating the celebrative mood.

Look for things to celebrate beyond birthdays, anniversaries, and national holidays. Celebrate new arrivals and births, deaths, rites of passage, accomplishments, new building consecration, beginnings and completions, visiting guests, trips, send outs for people leaving, unusual happenings, openings, new employees, recognition of people, beginning a day, ending of the day, beginning of the week, end of the week. Celebrations can be serious as well as joyous. The list is as endless as life and can be scheduled daily, weekly, and quarterly and still be flexible to include unexpected and happenings and occasions. Celebrations can be brief or lengthy. Celebrations nurture the community spirit with the simple joy of being alive.

E. THE SHARED MISSION

How many times have you heard of a parent testifying, "I could not have made it except for the fact that my children needed me to keep going." Having an important 'job' to do gives meaning, direction and purpose to every day living as well as inner strength in times of stress.

A shared mission unites a community in a steel bond of comradeship. Few things bind more strongly. One can even work effectively with someone s/he does not like if they share a common mission that is important to both of them. We can transcend personal discomfort for the sake of a valued mission. This can be witnessed in situations of conflict and in a situation where great struggle is required to realize a common goal.

The bonding is strengthened when the mission is a service to others. D.H. Lawrence reminds us, "Giving is still the truth about life . . . even if is only a man making a stool or a woman a pudding; if life goes into the pudding, good is the pudding, good is the stool; and we ripple with life through the days." Giving to others helps the giver as much as the receiver.

Some community organization strategists motivate a community by creating an enemy to attack who symbolizes an injustice to the community. Unfortunately this tactic often involves negative confrontational actions like protesting poor garbage service by dumping garbage on the front lawn of a city official in charge of that service. Such tactics rarely if ever produce long-range results. A common enemy is one way to motivate a community and illustrates the effectiveness of a common mission; but it is not the best way.

However, confrontations may be necessary at some point. If so, they must be done in a larger context and include caring for the 'enemy' that is being confronted as well as for the victims of the injustice. Genuine mission is always concerned for the well-being of the whole society. The tactics of Martin Luther King Jr. were effective not only because he used peaceful, non-violent confrontations but also because he cast them in the context of serving the oppressor as well as the oppressed, the whole nation and the global struggle for justice.

Only such a history-long, worldwide mission lays claim to the profound mystery that is a person's life. Only when that mission image is concretized in specific action does it come alive and become acted upon. The inclusive mission has to be incarnated in specific concrete action to breathe life into the image of mission, making it real. But no one campaign can become the all-defining mission. When the mission is reduced to a specific fight and that fight is won or lost; then the mission is over. Both dimensions, inclusive image and specific action, are needed for uniting a community in mission engagement.

One dimension of mission is to enable a community to understand their mission is to be the best community they can be for each other and for the sake of the world, to be a sign and symbol of possibility for the world. The family and community are the foundational building blocks of civilization. The health of the larger society depends on the health of the individual communities. To be a genuine community is in fact building civilization on behalf of the whole globe. It is building a better world, one community at a time. When one community makes it, others follow.

When one is aware that the well-being of the surrounding communities depends upon the health of one's own community s/he is motivated to improve the community, and is further motivated if his/her community can lead the way as a sign of possibility. When a community serves the larger society, its' culture is strengthened. In a mission of serving others the community life flourishes with value and meaning. A common mission catalyzes the overall development of a community.

F. UNENDING EDUCATION – FORMAL AND INFORMAL

A sixth major force for a vital community culture is structured, regular, on-going educational experiences for everyone. This was covered in Chapter IV: Education. It is here to remind us of its importance to the cultural life of the community. When we continue to grow intellectually, the intellect is nourished and our spirit remains bright. Our expenditure is replenished and balanced by the ingestion of new wisdom. We maintain a sense of being in control and continuing to grow. Burnout is avoided while the rigorous work continues. Continuing education helps keep the community alive and vibrant, fostering constant renewal. New learning is not only nourishment for the mind and spirit; it is also one of the most important sources of awakening that keeps us growing.

CONCLUSION

Recently the business world has become acutely aware of the impact that the culture of a company has on the bottom line and the general well-being of the business and its employees. The culture of a business enlivens or depresses the spirit and thus the productivity of the company. So companies have hired consultants to give their culture a boost, exploring options as varied as intentional décor, retreats, jungle stress events, experiences to create team spirit, uniform dress, and color in the workplace.

One company I spoke to closed down one of its most profitable sectors because the employees no longer experienced it as fulfilling for their lives. The major criterion for the decisions of that company is that work, which absorbs such a large amount of one's life, should first of all be fulfilling to the employees, and secondarily profitable to the company. Can you believe such a shift in the market place? A refreshing wind is blowing through the world.

Another company was locked into the 'production line' work of a factory. They initiated a program to give a sizable, yearly gift to help the larger society. Everyone in the company participated in nominating and choosing the recipient of the yearly gift. Representatives of the work force delivered the gift . The factory work took on a larger meaning beyond making a profit for the company and paying the employees a salary. The company prospered and the size of the gifts grew. The employees experienced themselves as serving a larger social purpose and the work became more meaningful.

We are in a cultural revolution, a time of redefining what it means to be a human being, ontologically and ethically. We are reinventing the symbols, style and wisdom of fulfilled living. Life is calling into question many of the assumptions of our ancestors about what it means to be a human being and what is the appropriate style of living that fulfills a life. We are reinventing human fulfillment. Hopefully we will preserve the genuine values of the past while refining and enlarging upon them.

The cultural life is the glue that holds the community together. Although it never exists apart from the economic and the political process, it is the most important factor in forming a community because it makes sense of sustaining and protecting the community. It is added value. Every part of the economic and political life is illuminated by the cultural life. Through the cultural processes the economic and political life becomes transparent to human values and meaning. The culture embodies the meaning of life together, the community's reason for being.

V. INDICATIVE PLANNING

A. The Practical Vision

B. The Underlying Contradictions

C. The Action Plan
1. Strategic Directions
2. Tactical Accomplishments
3. Implementation Plan

D. Monitoring Implementation

E. Consensus - the heart of planning

When one has a sufficient grasp of the situation through some beginning programs or actions, and enjoys a semblance of trust within the community, it is time to step back and build a common plan with the whole community. The best plan is always the one that is 'indicated' by the realities of the situation and the people impacted by the action plan.

An effective model of planning has three phases: (1) a five-year practical vision articulating the desired future of the community; (2) a depth analysis of what is blocking the realization of that vision; and (3) an action plan to pass through the blocks and realize the vision.

A. THE PRACTICAL VISION

Some formation processes erroneously begin by analyzing the problems in the community and creating plans to solve the problems. There are several problems with 'beginning with problems'.

The main issue is that one cannot discern real problems without a clear vision of the desired future. A problem is whatever is blocking the desired future; and so it is impossible to know the real problems before defining the vision. One young man thought his problem was that he did not have the degrees necessary to be the professor his father wanted him to be. When he woke up to the fact that he did not want to be a college professor, he realized that passing the PhD final exam was not a problem for him. What he needed was to go to flying school to become the pilot he always wanted to be. By beginning with the problems one is likely to miss the real problems which are illuminated only by the vision.

Secondly, one may assume that people want certain problems solved which they may not care about solving at the moment. We are inclined to begin by solving the problems 'we absolutely know' the community needs to solve, like unsafe drinking water. The community may not be aware of the value of safe drinking water; but they will want to stop their children from dying of dysentery. When they see that the block to their vision of healthy children is polluted drinking water; then they will want purified water, but not necessarily before.

Thirdly, lists of problems are likely to be numerous and demoralizing. Problems do not call people to action and motivate them. People commit themselves to a vision of a desired future. When there is a consensus about the desired future and what is blocking that vision, the community will energetically support whatever action is proposed to resolve the blocks to the vision.

The first planning step then is to enable the community to articulate its vision. Care and sensitivity are necessary because it may be difficult for a community to articulate its desired future if too many 'dreams have been deferred' again and again. The cumulative effect is to stop dreaming. A latent vision is always there; but the community may not be self-consciously aware of it.

To get the vision articulated, every community resident should have the opportunity to express their hopes and dreams. After every family has been canvassed, a representative voluntary group of residents can draw the vision together in a chart and a written statement. The vision needs to be 'practical' in that the community must be specific and concrete about what they desire. Ask the people, "What do you want to 'see in place' at the end of the next three to five years?" This question tends to get out specific, concrete images of a future that can be 'seen in the mind's eye' - a drip irrigation system, a new health center, electric lights, telephone service - rather than abstract concepts like better agriculture, or a healthier community, or better communication. A three to five-year time frame elicits more specific, concrete images than a ten or twenty-year dream.

Articulating and agreeing upon a vision has a powerful personal impact. The automatic and inevitable result of visioning is to call each individual to commit to realizing the vision. Interiorly, one is 'thrown outside oneself' to see oneself anew, disclosed in the 'light' of the newly stated vision. It requires one to take a new, decision about one's relationship to the community and to oneself in the light of the vision. One is required to decide to embrace and realize the vision which is to love one's community and one's self, or reject participating in realizing the vision. In this process of self-conscious decision, authentic selfhood emerges whenever one is able to choose to love one's life, i.e. to commit to the realization of the desired future.

This is another reason that it is sometimes difficult to get the vision stated. People realize intuitively that stating a vision places a demand upon their lives. In most cases the demand is welcomed. A new decision is taken for responsible action; and a general posture of responsible living is fostered. When the vision is embraced, it releases a flood of motivation.

When everyone sees that the whole community shares a common vision of the future, it foments a sense of unity in the community. The vision then becomes part of the common renewing story that the community tells themselves about who they are and why they are valuable.

The community can articulate a consensus about the five to ten major 'arenas' of their vision with two or four specific elements in each arena to ground the vision in practical images in as few as four hours using the methods the Institute of Cultural Affairs created to assist communities in their planning.

B. THE UNDERLYING CONTRADICTIONS

The second planning step is to analyze what is blocking the vision, to answer the question, "Why has the vision not been realized already?" What blocks the vision is called "contradiction" because it contradicts the vision.

Analyzing the contradictions begins by listing what is blocking each of the various parts of the vision. The blocks, when they are listed out, are then clarified so everyone is clear what each block title means. When the blocks from the various vision arenas are related together, it becomes obvious that many of the blocks from different vision arenas are similar and some may be basically the same thing. One begins to see that some blocks are blocking many parts of the vision. This narrows the focus toward discovering the few major blocks to the vision that are underneath the many blocks. These few blocks are seen as the major contradictions of the vision.

The grouping or 'gestalt' process should reveal three to seven major contradictions under the many problems. When the few underlying problems are resolved, multitudes of blocks are impacted, hence facilitating the realization of the entire vision.

The contradiction process treats the sickness, not the symptoms or the secondary results of the sickness. Over several months my uncle was treated for recurring earaches, headaches and sore throat. When he discovered the basic contradiction to his health was an infected tooth, it was pulled and all the other problems went away. Removing major contradictions is like removing my uncle's tooth.

When the contradictions are clarified, they are no longer seen as problems but as doorways to the desired future, and as such are not depressing. Rather, they provide a welcome and motivating challenge because they chart the way to a desired future. The action plans that attack the contradictions become more important than simply solving a list of problems; the plan becomes a healing balm for the community. The labor to resolve the contradictions is more significant and thus motivating. An added value is that the work becomes more organized and focused because the action plan will be dealing with few, clearly defined, basic, underlying problems.

C. THE ACTION PLAN

When the three to seven depth contradictions are identified, the analysis is done and the creation of the action plan can begin in earnest. The action plan consists of the strategic directions, the tactical accomplishments, and the implementing actions. The strategic plan is expressed as directions in which to move for the next two years to attack the contradictions and unblock the vision. The tactical accomplishments are specific, concrete, measurable action goals to be realized in the first year to move in the chosen strategic directions. The implementing actions describe detailed, specific steps for specific persons to do at a specific time, in a specific place, in the first three months to begin to realize the tactical accomplishments. These actions will resolve the contradictions and bring the vision to fruition.

An effective action plan has three parts: (1) a strategy that delineates general directions to follow for two years to move through the blocks, (2) a one-year tactical action plan that defines specific accomplishments needed to facilitate movement in the strategic directions for the first year, and (3) an implementing plan that spells out in detail what must be done the first ninety days toward realizing the tactical goals of the year.

1. Strategic Directions

The first part of the action plan is to define the broad, inclusive directions in which the community must move to begin to resolve the contradictions and release the desired future. These major directions delineate rationally and intuitively what needs to happen in the next two years toward resolving the contradictions. They give guidance, perspective, focus and systemic organization to the action plan.

After listing many, many actions that could be taken to attack the contradictions, similar actions are then grouped together forming 8 to 12 groupings. Look at each group of actions and discern the arena of actions that they represent. For example one group may be in the arena of health, another the arena of construction, etc. When eight to twelve action arenas have been identified then study the actions listed under each arena of actions and group the actions into three or four major dimensions of the action arena and title the 3 or four sub-points of the action arena. Then title the action arena to hold the general concept of all the actions listed . Give each action arena a three or four word title that summarizes the actions listed and defines the direction the community needs to move in each action arena, for example 'Total Community Health Care', or 'Medical Service for All.' These will be the direction that the community needs to move to resolve the contradictions.

Then, in the same manner the eight to twelve action directions are grouped in similar way and titled to discern and define the three or four overarching and unifying strategic directions that are indicated by the groupings of the action directions. Each of the three or four overarching strategic directions then has two to four sub-directions to give substance and specific grounding to the discerned overarching strategic directions.

This gestalt into strategic directions gives unity and focus to the tactical and implementing parts of the action plan. It also gives more flexibility for maneuvering since one can alter the actions 'in flight' with the guidance of the strategic directions. They provide a radar like system to guide the flight of the action plan. If new actions move more effectively in the charted directions, one is free to change the plan in flight. It also provides the course correction to check if the accomplishments are moving in the correct direction.

Having the focus of a few strategic directions allows more concentration of resources and increases effective action because more things can be done at once and actions have multiple impacts. It's like going to town to do ten things at once rather then going to town ten times to do one thing. It gets more done per trip; and each action has multiple impacts.

2. Tactical Accomplishments
The tactical plan identifies the major accomplishments that need to be realized in the first year to move in the strategic directions. The accomplishments must pass the SAMS test in that they must be specific, accomplishable, measurable and schedulable.

- **Specific** – concrete action goals, the end result can be visualized, seen in the mind's eye.
- **Accomplishable** – realizable, possible to complete in one year or less
- **Measurable** – quantifiable so that success of the plans can be measured, so one can know whether or not the accomplishment is realized and someone can be held accountable.
- **Schedulable** - can be scheduled and phased for completion in an estimated amount of time frame of not more than one year.

Some actions listed in the strategy session can now be recovered in the accomplishments brainstorm. The two planning segments support each other. The planning now begins to dialogue between strategies and tactical actions to correct, amplify, and improve the plan. Effective thinking always employs a process of going back and forth from the specific to the comprehensive and back to the particular.

Projected accomplishments are specific, accomplishable, quantifiably measurable, and can be placed on a one-year calendar and assigned to an individual or persons to be responsible for getting it done. They move the community in the strategic directions that are necessary to pass through the contradictions and realize the common vision.

3. Implementation Plan
The third part of the action plan is to decide how to effectively implement a well defined part of each tactical accomplishment during the next 90 days. The implementation plans spell out what is to be done each week, how it will be done, who will do it, where it is to be done, and why do it anyway. At the end of 90 days another 90-day plan is created to continue to implement the tactical actions.

To create a plan of implementing actions requires a special kind of thinking and skill to visualize a three-month journey of actions toward realizing the accomplishments. One has to foresee how to breakdown the tasks into doable bits that take a day or less to do so the implementing action can be assigned to a particular week in a twelve week plan. It is the small, very specific actions that can be put in sequential order and then placed on a weekly schedule. Implementation plans tell what needs to be done on a specific day at 9:00 AM at a specific location in order to prepare for what needs be done the next day and the next until the tactical accomplishment is completed. Answering who, what, when, why, and how are the guides posts for the adequacy of the implementation plan. The implementation plan lays out detailed actions in sequential order that actualize the accomplishments.

Many plans break down at the point of asking what is to be done tomorrow at 8:00 AM and the next ninety tomorrows. It is the nitty-gritty action planning that insures victory. It is General Simon Bolivar pulling the nails out of the church pews so his army could make the ammunition needed for the next days battle.

Winning is in attention to the details. When goals are not realized, it is usually because planning stops before creating an adequate implementing plan. Sometimes implementation plans are completely missing, leaving the workers to fly by the seat of their intuitive pants.

Three months is as long as one can project implementing actions because that is as long as one can effectively schedule detailed actions. Many people have trouble imagining actions past two weeks, so all the implementing actions end up scheduled for the first two or three weeks of the 90 days. It would be very difficult to imagine implementing actions for more than a 90-day period; but one could make a case for going with 60-day implementation planning.

A second reason for limiting the plan to 90 days is that many things change in 90 days, giving one a new context in which to operate. Factors outside the plan may present a new reality with which to deal. Or the change may come from the actualization of the plans that alters the reality. The implementation plan may go faster or slower than anticipated and so adjustments are needed. Some planned actions may be block and have to be redesigned.

When change occurs – and it always does – then new plans are needed. So implementation planning is done for three months and then redone for the following three months. Adjustments are also made weekly to accommodate change in one's situation. Plans are guides for weekly maneuvering, not chains to limit one's action. Plans exist to free one to act more intentionally, be more flexible, creative, intuitive and comprehensive. A plan is a place from which to stand to decide what to do in any given moment. Re-planning is a yearly, quarterly, monthly, weekly and daily activity. Recreate the implementing plan each 90 days and adjust weekly and daily.

D. MONITORING IMPLEMENTATION

After the implementing actions are listed, placed in sequential order and placed on a timeline, one must be able to monitor the actualization of the many implementing actions in the plan. This can be done by designating the key action of the week for each arena of action. The assumption is that if it gets done, likely all the others will have been done. So by checking to see if the key actions are done one can monitor fairly well the progress and intuit how well the whole plan is being realized. The morale of the troops is another indicator. It is high if the plan is being realized.

E. CONSENSUS – THE HEART OF PLANNING

The people's commitment to implementing the plan is shaped largely by the quality and depth of the consensus created in the planning process. Commitment is built into the consensus process. It is part and parcel of making a consensus. It lays a claim on those participating and forms a unity of purpose. Stewing through discussions to form consensus creates a plan to which people find themselves naturally committed. They wake up willingly committed at the end of the planning.

Consensus builds commitment far better than majority rule. When we vote to reach a decision, those who voted against the plan often feel that it is not their plan. They may even proclaim that they are not responsible to see that the plan gets done. But when the group builds a plan by consensus, even those who disagree with the plan are committed to actualize the plan, because they have agreed to the consensus of the group of which they are a part and to whom they are committed. Therefore they acquiesce to the will of the group. In the 'act of consensus' everyone experiences that they are responsible to the group for implementing the plan. Commitment to the group commits them to participate in realizing the plan.

If a group decides on a plan and one is convinced it is the consensus of the group (that all positions have been heard and honored by serious consideration and the decision is in fact the will of the group), then one is motivated to acquiesce and commit oneself to the plan, although disagreeing with the chosen action. Even if the plan is diametrically contrary to one's own best wisdom, one commits to the group's decision as though it were one's own best wisdom. Submitting to the consensus, while disagreeing with the content, indicates trust in the group's wisdom, which honors and affirms the group. The community is more important than one's opinion on any given action or subject.

Often the consensus process produces a third alternative to opposing views that leads to a better solution than either beginning position. However if the consensus of the group violates one's moral stance, then one cannot acquiesce in the decision and needs to leave the group and/or fight to reverse the consensus. Voiding the consensus breaks one's covenant with the group.

Either way the commitment to the community remains, if only in the decision to stand over against the community for the sake of the community's well-being.

The consensus process commits everyone to the entire plan because consensus assumes a covenant (implied or stated) between the individual and the community. One comes to consensus through a covenantal trust of the group and a consensus process creates or deepens covenantal relationship.

Creating community is a process of moving from existing to deeper levels of covenant. A few words here about covenant may be helpful to understanding the process of creating community. I want to make the case that communities can create covenants that have all the aspects that we normally assign to the love-covenant between two people.

A covenant involves two or more individuals in profound love for one another, where love is defined as the act of valuing the other, that is, to place the well-being of the other above or equal to one's own well-being. Love is a verb, the action of valuing the other in and of his/herself, apart from what they say, feel, do, or think. The valuing does not depend on their usefulness, their function or their agreement with you. The controlling concern is the overarching value placed by each on the other. Since it is important to preserve the other, one seeks to live out of consensus, which honors the other's beliefs and opinions. Consensus is seeing the wonder-filled mystery that is the other and choosing to value the other's opinions even when disputing them.

Love here is not necessarily a feeling but an action and may even be accompanied by a hostile feeling. A loving act, however, can transform a hostile emotion to an positive emotion that may not be present before the act which works the transformation. Thus building consensus, seen as 'a loving action', can create the positive emotion usually attributed to the word 'love' within a group of individuals who are in diametric disagreement about the decision being taken. Authentic community is the expression and incarnation of the love act of building consensus

Consensus assumes covenant and covenant arises out of the consensus process. Covenant desires consensus with the covenanted one. They are two sides of a coin. One comes to consensus through the covenantal trust, stated or implied. The consensus process nurtures and deepens covenant relationships because it honors and values the group. The unity of a covenanted group rests on the mutual act of cherishing the being of the other, apart from the agreeing or disagreeing.

Of course, one takes care to insure that the right plan is created for the community, but submits to the wisdom of the group until one can change the consensus with a 'better' plan. While submitting to the will and desires of the other, the option is always open to persuade the group that one's own idea or position is best for the group.

The community that operates out of consensus will find the people united and committed to the plan in ways not understandable by those who use other processes of deciding. Indicative planning honors all who participate. It gives to all the option of deciding the future of their lives. It is a genuine expression of love of oneself and the community.

CREATING COMMUNITY

The Tenfold Path to Community Creation

1. Nurture those who care in the community and enable them to be effective with enabling structures. This is the way to long lasting, self-sustaining development.

2. Formulate a liberating story of significance. This is the best way to care for those who care and engage people in caring for the community.

3. Engage everyone in direct actions of care for the community. This is the key to develop and deepen commitment to the community.

4. Continually awaken new awareness. This enlivens the imagination and fosters self-esteem, spiritual development, and responsibility.

5. Demonstrate new possibility. This inspires courage and hope for an open future.

6. Interchange knowing, doing and being. This deepens relationships with one another, fostering genuine community of mutual respect and trust.

7. Foster a learning community for everyone. This feeds minds and spirits.

8. Be as inclusive and integrally comprehensive as possible. This balances the economic, political and cultural dynamics, a key to community health and sustainable development. Think globally and act locally. With a global context intensify action on your particular situation.

9. Involve increasing numbers in deciding their future through consensus planning. This creates responsible citizens who experience owning the plan and the community.

10. Stand at relaxed attentiveness to the Now, as the forgiven one, trusting the wisdom of the community and creation, 'to weigh up and direct the course of history'.

One recreated community enriches all communities. It is a beacon of hope, a role model to follow. It multiples and populates the earth with authentic human beings capable of living to their fullest potential. There is no neutral ground in the sphere of basic human need. One is either for it or against it. To ignore the need is the same as acting against it. One seeks community or negates it by neglect. One is either creating or destroying community. One is either a positive or negative force. So work at it. Go forth and be proactive; seek community; pay for the privilege. If we do not do it, that's okay too. Someone will be raised up who will do it; and the rest will follow in their tracks. Whoever creates the model of the future will be in charge, and illuminate the future that civilization will seek to follow.

ADDENDUM ONE

Sample Matrix For Maintaining The Political Frame

	FRIEND	ADVOCATE	GUARDIAN
Government Sector			
Private Sector - Business - Professional			
Religious Sector			
NGO Sector			
Medical Sector			
Other sectors			

ADDENDUM TWO

Sample Group Brainstorm To Create Community Stories

Context: To create some poetry that holds the value and self-understanding of community members, let us take ten minutes to individually brainstorm data. There are no right or wrong answers to the questions below and no one is going to know who wrote what lines. Please do not stop and think; just write the first thing that pops into your mind.

1. What is the first thing that comes to your mind when you hear the word *(name of community)*?
2. What do you find yourself missing when you are away from *(name of community)*?
3. When you are away from this community, what do you think or wonder about?
4. Complete the following sentence in three to five words: *(name of community)* is like _____
5. Imagine you are an abstract painter painting a picture of *(name of community)*. What would be the dominant color of the painting?
6. If a non-resident friend asked you, "What is so great about *(name of community)*," how would you answer your friend (in three to five words)?
7. In five words or less say, "What is it about *(name of community)* that makes life better for you? What is it about this community that makes life better for everyone?"
8. Imagine you are leaving *(name of community)*, never to return. Just before you leave, "What would be your parting words to the land? to the people?"
9. Imagine you have made a movie about life in *(name of community)* and now must give it a title. "What would be the title of your movie?"
10. Why did you choose *(name of community)* to live?

Thank you for your responses. We will use them to create a poem, song or story to celebrate the significance of living in (name of community).

With this brainstorm we can take phrases and use them to write poetry about the community or put the words to an existing tune known by all.

BIBLIOGRAPHY

Berdgall, Terry D. (1993). *Methods for Active Participation: Experiences in Rural Development from East and Central Africa.* Nairobi: Oxford University Press.

Boulding, Kenneth. (1956). *The Image.* Ann Arbor, MI: University of Michigan Press.

Bohm, David. (1980). *Wholeness and the Implicate Order.* NewYork: Routledge.

Burbidge, John. (1997). *Beyond Prince and Merchant: Citizen Participation and the Rise of Civil Society.* New York: PACT Press.

Drucker, Peter. (1993). *Post-Capitalist Society.* New York: HarperBusiness.

Fox, Mathew. (1994). *The Reinvention of Work: A New Vision of Livelihood in Our Time.* San Francisco: Harper.

Friedman, Thomas L. (1999). *The Lexus and the Olive Tree, Understanding Globalization.* New York: Farrar, Straus, Giroux.

Friedman, Thomas L. (2006). *The World is Flat: A brief history of the 21st Century.* New York: Farrar, Straus & Giroux.

Gardner, Howard. (1983). *Frames of Mind: the Theory of Multiple Intelligences.* New York: Harper & Row Publishing.

Harman, Willis. (1986). "Transformed leadership: Two contrasting concepts." In J. D. Adams (Ed.), *Transforming leadership from vision to results.* Alexandria, VA: Miles River Press.

Hawken, Paul & Lovins, Amory and Hunter. (1999). *Natural Capitalism.* New York: Little Brown and Co.

Henderson, Hazel. (1991). *Paradigms in Progress.* Indianapolis: Knowledge Systems, Inc.

Hughes, Langston. (1995). *The Collected Poems of Langston Hughes.* Arnold Rampersad, Editor. London: Vintage Classics.

Huntington, Samuel P. (1996). *The Clash of Civilizations and the Remaking of World Order.* New York: Simon & Schuster.

ICA Brussels. (1988). *Approaches That Work in Rural Development.* IERD Series No. 3. Munich: K. G. Saur.

Jenkins, Jon. (1996). *The International Facilitator's Companion.* Groningen, the Netherlands: Imaginal Training.

Kant, I. (1950). *Critique of Pure Reason.* New York: Humanities Press.

Kierkegaard, S. (1954). *Fear and Trembling.* Garden City, NY: Doubleday & Company Inc.

Kloepfer, John. (1990), *The Art of Formative Questioning: A way to foster self-disclosure.* Ann Arbor, MI: UMI.

Korten, David C. and Klass, Rudi. (1984). *People Centred Development: Contributions Toward Theory and Planning of Development.* West Hartford: Kumarian Press.

Lawrence, D.H. (1989). *The Selected Poems of D. H. Lawrence.* London: Penguin Books

Lazear, David. (1991). *Seven Ways of Knowing: Teaching for Multiple Intelligences.* New York: Skylight Publishing.

Lerner, Michael. (1996). *The Politics of Meaning.* Don Mills, ON: Addison-Wesley Publishing Co.

Rifkin, Jeremy. (1996). *The End of Work.* New York: Tarcher/ Putnam.

Mathews, Joseph Wesley. (1965) *Religious Studies I.* New Orleans: Ecumenical Institute unpublished manuscript.

Nelson, Jo. (2000). *The Art of Focused Conversation for Schools: Over 100 Ways to Guide Clear Thinking and Promote Learning.* Toronto: Canadian Institute of Cultural Affairs.

Quinn, Daniel. (1992). *Ishmael: An Adventure of the Mind and Spirit.* New York: Bantam/Turner Books.

Russell, Peter. (1995). *The Global Brain Awakens: Our next evolutionary leap.* Palo Alto, CA: Peter Russell

Senge, Peter M. (1990). *The Fifth Discipline, The Art and Practice of the Learning Organization.* New York: Currency Press.

Spencer, Laura J. (1989). *Winning Through Participation: Meeting the Challenge of Corporate Change with the Technology of Participation.* Dubuque: Kendall/Hunt Publishing Company.

Stanfield, R. Brian. (2002). *The Workshop Book: from Individual Creativity to Group Action. Toronto:* The Canadian Institute of Cultural Affairs.

Stanfield, R. Brian, General Editor. (1997). *The Art of Focused Conversation: 100 ways to Access Group wisdom in the workplace.* Toronto: Canadian Institute of Cultural Affairs.

Stanfield, R. Brian, (2004). *The Courage to Lead.* Toronto: Canadian Institute of Cultural Affairs.

Troxel, James P., (Ed.) (1995). *Government Works: Profiles of People Making a Difference.* Alexandria, Virginia: Miles River Press.

Troxel, James P., (Ed.) (1993). *Participation Works: Business Cases from Around the world.* Alexandria, Virginia: Miles River Press.

Williams, R. Bruce. (1993). *More Than Fifty ways to Build Team Consensus.* Palatine, IL: IRI/ Skylight Publishing.

van Kaam, A. (1975). *In Search of Spiritual Identity.* Denville, NJ: Dimension Books.

Zakaria, Fareed. (2009). *The Post American World.* New York: W.W. Norton & Company.